The People of Nineteenth Street

Sherry Scott

Black Rose Writing | Texas

© 2018 by Sherry Scott
All rights reserved. No part of this book may be reproduced, stored in a retrieval system or transmitted in any form or by any means without the prior written permission of the publishers, except by a reviewer who may quote brief passages in a review to be printed in a newspaper, magazine or journal.

The author grants the final approval for this literary material.

First printing

Some names and identifying details may have been changed to protect the privacy of individuals.

ISBN: 978-1-68433-190-1
PUBLISHED BY BLACK ROSE WRITING
www.blackrosewriting.com

Printed in the United States of America
Suggested Retail Price (SRP) $16.95

The People of Nineteenth Street is printed in Chaparral Pro

To my parents, Vinson and Fay Shields,
for providing my story and to all those who have intersected it.

Acknowledgments

I would first like to thank my editor, Stephanie Lane, for her dedication and professional guidance. Your agreement to take on another one of my projects is enough to keep me believing; you make me better than I am.

Thanks to David and Ginger Cook, for sharing their love of art and the photographs provided. It was synchronous bliss the day I walked into your showing Ginger, and immediately connected with your artistic take on an era gone by. Thank you for helping me live my vision.

Thank you to my immediate family for supporting and putting up with my distant dreaming. Cliff Scott, you make all this possible; your loyalty and love is irreplaceable. Madison, Tyler and Aubry, you are my dreams. Aaron, you have been a part of my story through good and bad; you'll always be in my heart. To my dad, who has soldiered on alone these many years, I am indebted to you and mom for a home that allowed a fantasy-envisioned childhood that has brightened many a dark day in the remembering.

A special thanks to all the educators in my life, good or bad; the experience taught me more. And for all those who have somehow intertwined their story with this life tale, whether in the passing moment or long narrative, you've enriched its essence. Thank you; you made it worth telling.

The People of
Nineteenth Street

Contents

Prologue

Chapter 1 - The People of Nineteenth Street　　11

Chapter 2 - The Best Day of My Life　　21

Chapter 3 - Burl and Opal　　31

Chapter 4 - People Next Door　　45

Chapter 5 - Just a Clean Up Woman　　57

Chapter 6 - Thirty Days in a Nursing Home　　64

Chapter 7 - Living with Mental Illness　　72

Chapter 8 - Standing on the Corner　　87

Chapter 9 - The Eighth Floor　　96

Chapter 10 - Way Behind on *Rent*　　106

Chapter 11 - Through the Back Door　　116

Chapter 12 - Coming Full Circle　　131

About the Author

Prologue

In the year my mother died, someone sent me an email that was meant to be read and then forwarded for some automated blessing. The amount of blessing corresponded to the number of people who responded and forwarded the message.

People come into your life for a reason, a season or a lifetime...
When someone is in your life for a REASON, it is usually to meet a need you have expressed. Some people come into your life for a SEASON, because your turn has come to share, grow or learn. They may teach you something you have never done.
Lifetime relationships teach you lifetime lessons, things you must build upon in order to have a solid emotional foundation...

Blah, blah, blah
The comfort I found in the message was something far removed from its purpose; it was validation I wasn't being foolish.
What had started as an escape during that time became a total and irrevocable obsession. I had a crush on a rock star from my youth; someone to whom I had not paid that much attention during his rock-glam years. But during the mid-life crunch following the death of my mother, his music, his face, his past came crashing into my reality until each awakening day greeted me with a song of his spinning in my head. And that was just the beginning. So trapped in the world of visualizing my new invented self into his past, I began to separate and close myself off to those closest to me, primarily my family. I still functioned but only so long as I was somewhere else in my head.
At the time, I wasn't interested in my lifetime relationships; I had lost one, and the others were beginning to feel like a burden. This email message signaled that I might find purpose in this madness. I wasn't being self-centered, eccentric or even going crazy; this 1974 elusive figure was taking me somewhere, though I had no idea where or why.
In time, this obsession passed, but not until I had learned its objective. I reclaimed my passion for expressing myself through the pen. Poetry and prose were rekindled. In the words of Julia Cameron in *The Artist's Way,* "People heal because creativity is healthy—and practicing it, they find their

greater selves." Through my writing, my past and its forgotten gems of rock collections, childhood playmates and early summer mornings were recalled and "re-treasured." The people associated with those times came back with roaring clarity; their contributions and mere presence had shaped who I was, whether they deemed it so or not.

People from my past, whether close or afar, are often remembered without name, place or incident association; they simply exist. I find they often invade my conscious thinking and sometimes my dreams without an explanation, or at least one that I can ascertain. But I claim them just the same.

More beautifully put than I can write is the example of a remembered face in the late, great Rosalind Russell autobiography, *Life is a Banquet*. While the famous film and stage star was busy paying homage to the stars at Metro-Goldwyn-Mayer Studios, her dear friend Frank Sinatra or her closest family members, she sprinkled tributes throughout her book to the nameless who made just as notable impacts on her life and career. Having read the book myself years ago, I was particularly struck by a moving encounter that took place early in her stage acting career while working with a summer stock company in Saranac Lake, New York.

> "She pulled a cord, which lit a bare bulb hanging over a round wooden table in the middle of the floor, and she boiled water on a hot plate in the corner. She had one cup and one spoon, and she brought me tea in the cup and drank hers from a glass. Then she brought out a tiny white cylinder and put it down in front of me… It was a cupcake. All that woman's salary—and it was meager—went to support her niece, but she couldn't let my birthday pass without my having a party, so she'd spent fifteen or twenty cents for the cake. And she didn't own two cups.
>
> Years later I saw her walking across Broadway, and we stopped and talked. She's long since gone to the old actresses' heaven, but I still think of that party. She gave me the dearest birthday of my life."

Rosalind Russell once sat next to Winston Churchill as his designated dinner guest at the American Embassy in England, hosted by the U.S. ambassador, Joseph Kennedy, and his wife, Rose. Yet, she gave just as much, if not more, tribute to this aging character actress who lived in a four-flight, walk-up boarding house than to the famous "greats" in her life.

It is to this end I have written this book: to pay homage to those who have come in and out of my life for however brief or long a time. Some I knew intimately, and others I never even knew by name. I trust that a reason existed for our meeting; for why else would their memory reside in the corridors of time sealed off, seldom unlocked or visited. But, oh, it's been fun recounting persons and times that have brightened a gray day with just an intrusive thought.

Chapter 1
The People of Nineteenth Street

My affinity for older people may stem from my being surrounded by them for as long as I can remember. My earliest playmates, other than my parents, were the elderly living on and around Nineteenth Street. Mrs. Wilson lived next door, and my best friend, Karen Hampton, lived down the block, but I wager to say I spent more time plowing through Mrs. Wilson's blue hydrangea bushes to get to her back door than walking down the street to play with Karen. I know so, because I left a trail through her flower bed, and she waged an intense campaign to divert me to her front door to save the hydrangeas.

I knew the pre-stroke and the post-stroke Mrs. Wilson. Though two different people, I'm sure that the latter was more endeared to me, for I was old enough to remember her as such. I have one early memory of sitting on her lap while out on her back porch overlooking her immense vegetable garden. She wore a dark print dress of silky fabric, and I felt content there. That is the only memory I have of close contact with her. Flash forward through images of time I retained, and the garden becomes a blank tablet of dirt that the grass eventually covers. No more picking or shelling and certainly no more sitting on the back porch. They may as well have sealed that back door, for it was never used again. And then enters Mrs. Early and an array of changes that I remember best about my old friend.

Mrs. Early stayed with Mrs. Wilson during the weekdays; another woman came on the weekends. She drove a two-toned, white and fuchsia humpty car (everyone drove humpty cars back then), had thick glasses that made her eyes look like small black cannonballs and was hard of hearing. My dad used to make remarks about "the blind leading the blind next door." I was too young to understand the reference he was making until the ambulance showed up one night in Mrs. Wilson's driveway.

Some sort of "spell" had prompted Mrs. Wilson to call for an ambulance and my parents. When my parents arrived, Mrs. Early was seated on the couch, somewhat incoherent, with her head propped back and eyes closed. My dad got right down in her face and yelled, "Mrs. Early, do you know where you are?" With both cannonballs firing back in his face, she replied, "I'm fine! Do you know who you are?" Shortly thereafter, I didn't see Mrs. Early or her car anymore. Other visitors still dropped in on Mrs. Wilson from time to time, not including the Fuller Brush man, who came to visit our house as well.

Every so often, a man dressed in a suit stopped by to walk Mrs. Wilson and her high-topped black shoes up and down the front porch steps very slowly. Holding her by the arm, he appeared business-like and patient all at the same time. I watched from the front yard next door and stayed out of the way, for Mom must have mentioned the word "therapist" to me at some point. The only other times I saw her outside was when her fishing buddy showed up in her turquoise 1950s model Chevrolet pickup truck. (Mrs. Wilson had fished avidly at one time.)

She was a tall brunette sporting a straw hat who never did seem to go into the house. She seemed content to stand alongside her truck or sit in the driver's seat with the door propped open while talking to Mrs. Wilson; the smell of fish could explain her reluctance in going any farther than the front drive. The bed of the truck held fishing poles with little red bobbers on the ends, Styrofoam chests for the bait and fish, a mixture of nets and a tackle box. Whether they talked shop or not, the conversation seemed to be intense and enjoyed by both, even though the days of Mrs. Wilson's joining her friend on the lake were in the past.

Mrs. Wilson remained my closest *older* friend, but I made the rounds in the neighborhood to visit others on a regular basis, much to my mother's chagrin—she said I never knew when it was time to come home. Mrs. Windom lived in the white frame house on the corner of Nineteenth and Austin Streets just like us; she lived across Austin Street, which ran along the north side of our house. She drove a long, black and white car and always looked like she was dressed for some important job such as a secretary or someone behind the counter of an insurance office or bank. Because she worked, I didn't visit much with Mrs. Windom, but she once boarded a woman who made and sold Barbie doll clothes. Though I don't recall her name, I remember her room, the way she wore her hair, where she moved after she left Mrs. Windom's house, and, most importantly, the clothes she made for sale that she kept in a large box underneath her bed.

Now, my granny had made Barbie doll dresses for me from Simplicity or McCall patterns out of material scraps she had left over from dresses or aprons she had made for herself, and they were okay, but this was something else. This woman sewed beautiful ball gowns out of yellow chiffon with netting overlay and decorated the bodice with jewelry studs. It was one thing when you handed your grandmother a pattern with a wedding dress on the cover, and it came back finished in a black synthetic print like the cape the hairdresser threw around you to keep the hair off your clothes, and quite another thing to behold the most beautiful fabrics and styles befitting a ten-inch doll with extremely high arches. She would pull out the big white dress box from under the bed, and some of the other girls from around the block and I would ooh and aah over the different outfits, vowing to come back when we had saved enough money to purchase our favorite selection. When the time came, I couldn't make up my mind and bought two or three of the more conservative pieces as opposed to the gorgeous gowns over which I had salivated. It was just too much; perhaps I had become accustomed to the down-to-earth approach and style of my granny.

Mrs. Windom must have been proficient at taking care of self and home. She worked full time, raised a garden, kept her yard groomed, and boarded not just one renter but two. The woman who made and sold doll clothes lived in a room in Mrs. Windom's for a short while, but I was far better acquainted with her other renter. Mr. Bridges lived in a little two-room white framed house next to Mrs. Windom's garage. It looked like an afterthought of a house, more like a storage building or a shed, but it did have a kitchen. Mr. Bridges was an old widower who lived alone and was probably in Paris due to the town's proximity to the Veterans Administration hospital in the neighboring town of Bonham, Texas. He was about the same height as my mom (short) and walked with a little stiff, bow-legged gait. He wore dark brown creased pants, white or tan cotton short-sleeve shirts, tucked in, and always wore a fedora style hat while outside or when going into town.

An old friend of his who would drop in occasionally to visit drove a four-door black 1949 Ford. Its humpty rear end with its little oblong tail lights made me almost feel sorry for it. On rainy days when I had to bring my red tricycle in the house, I'd ride up and down the halls of my house and park my little black Ford with its beady tail lights in my mom's closet while I visited with my old friend. I felt like pretending *poor*. What I didn't realize at the time was that these two were old World War I veterans; Mr. Bridges' friend walked with a wooden crutch and drove over from the retired veterans' home in Bonham.

Mr. Bridges cooked differently than my mom, so I used to go over and sit on a stool in his little kitchen and watch him while he prepared his supper. For one thing, he left the skin on his potatoes while cutting them in quarters to fry, and, instead of using butter sticks that came in a package of four, he cooked with a great big block of butter. He called it "railroad butter." But I must have misunderstood him, for he was probably referring to the individual servings of butter that were common in railroad dining cars, sliced from a block of butter and served in small bowls of thick china—"butter pats."

It didn't seem strange or inappropriate to him—or my mom, for that matter—that I would go over to his house uninvited and/or unannounced to spend time, check out his little garden out back or watch him fry-cook. (Of course, my mom may not have been aware of all the time I spent there and certainly would have not approved of my overstaying my welcome.) I would sit in his front room, where he slept as well, and listen to him drone on about his grandkids until I would get bored and have to leave in search of someone else to visit or some other more compelling activity. I wonder if Mr. Bridges' bragging could have been responsible for getting him into some trouble.

One night after returning home from somewhere, we noticed a red four-door sedan parked on the street in front of our house with a man sitting in the driver's seat. My dad questioned if it was James, Mrs. Wilson's grown son, but from the light of the street lamp we clearly saw it was not as we slowly made our way up the drive. I stared intently at the man from the backseat window. The next morning, I learned from my mom that the man had robbed Mr. Bridges. During a time when most people slept with open windows and screened doors that may or may not have been latched, the man stole Mr. Bridges' money at gunpoint while the rest of the block slept soundly. I thought about the mauve-colored ceramic jar that Mr. Bridges would proudly show me, filled to the brim with half dollars he was saving to give to his grandkids. I wondered how that man could have known. Whether he had more money stashed in his humble abode than what he showed me I will never know, for so traumatized by a stranger coming in on him in the middle of the night, he soon moved to be closer to his family. I don't recall seeing him again after that night but would sometimes lay awake thinking about poor Mr. Bridges, alone in the dark with the face of that blond-haired man lit by the corner street light robbing him of his grandchildren's coins and peace of mind.

Peace of *another* kind of mind was something I didn't quite understand yet, or I took for granted. Another man I talked with from time to time lived in the neighborhood, one street over from ours. He would often walk by himself in the evenings and would stop and talk to us kids during our outside play and games. He wore khaki slacks and white or light print cotton short-sleeve shirts, untucked, thick brown sandals with white socks, dark-rimmed glasses and parted his hair to the side. He appeared older than my dad, because he walked so slowly. Years later, when I heard comedian Robert Klein describe the tell-tale sign of a Puerto Rican on the streets of New York with his Guayabera shirts and brown sandals always worn with thick white socks, I thought of him. I noticed something different about him, though the difference my mom noticed was more ominous than his attire.

One hot summer day on my way back from the neighborhood store I stopped by his house to pay him a visit. He lived in a little white frame bungalow that sported a large tuft of pampas grass by the front steps and a huge water cooler that hummed loudly and dripped cold water down the front. I figured the sound of the water cooler must have deafened my repeated knocks on the door since he didn't answer, so I sat on his front porch for a while before deciding to move on. My mother and I were driving through the old neighborhood decades later when I pointed to his house and relayed the story of trying to visit him. My mother about stroked, "He had some mental illness; I always thought there was something strange about the way he would stop and talk to you kids. I would have died if I would have known you were going over there by yourself!" It had seemed like a perfectly natural way to spend the hot afternoon to me.

I always seemed to find other open doors, or should I say, open *ears*. An elderly couple lived around the corner in a frame house with black shutters and a front door that opened onto a porch that looked out on two peach trees in the front yard. I never recall being invited inside, but I would sit and visit with them in the late afternoon while they sat in their ladder-back wooden chairs, to the point of forgetting what time it was and arriving late for dinner. My mother would repeat, "You never know when to come home," a phrase she used regarding my poor sense of timing up through my high school years and beyond. It was easy for me to forget home when right across the street from the modest frame stood the Fendley car garage.

Heaven on earth denotes a place of rapture and bliss, which is exactly what the Fendleys' house, yard, and garage for auto repair, held for me. I was a regular visitor at the home's address on the corner of Nineteenth Southwest and Kaufman Streets. To call Darren Fendley's dad a working man would have been putting it lightly. I never saw him without his slate blue matching trousers and work shirt on, covered in grease, and a red mechanic's rag sticking out of his back pocket. He had a large crop of black hair on top of the head he continuously had stuck under the hood of some car on which he was working. He was so busy that he never seemed to notice three kids intently playing around in the grease and soot out behind the garage like we had just discovered the ultimate playground.

Darren was a dark-haired boy a year or two older than I was but who was short for his age; we were eye level and got along just fine. Mary, a lovely blonde-headed girl with soft curls and blue cat-eye glasses, was the same age as Darren and lived two doors down from him on Kaufman Street. They had known each other longer, but they let me play along just the same. For a time, it became a ritual to meet at Darren's after school where we would cook up (or pretend to cook) some concoction of soot, dirt and grease stirred by all the sticks we could find out back of the garage. It was fascinating. In our neighborhood, people still burned their own trash in large metal barrels in their backyards. We had a large blue and yellow striped barrel that was placed at the back of our property. There was so much trash burned at the Fendleys' that they had multiple cans: we always had a fresh mound of ashes to mix in with all the other inherent wastes found outside a working car garage. We vowed that, come December, instead of traditional Christmas toys, we would be perfectly happy with a sack of switches and soot if Santa so chose because of our bad behavior.

As cool as the ambience of Mr. Fendley's garage was, the house and yard proved just as intriguing. The spacious green lawn wrapped around the house, ambled some distance out back and stood next to a barbed-wire fenced lot on the north side of the house, where a horse was sometimes kept. The house fronted Nineteenth Street, which was a busy road marked like a highway that ran north and south through the west end of town. The road traveled on to Lake Crook, if you traveled far enough north, and, just down the road from the Fendleys' heading south out of town, it led to the huge B & W plant. The plant would account for the stream of cars that traveled our street and especially for the big Red Ball trucks that used to scare me to death. With no sidewalk out front, the driveway in front of the house was my only thoroughfare for driving my red tricycle. Around and around I traveled to and from the grocery store, the drive-through window at the bank (warning kids in the backseat to behave), and the gas station for $2 worth of regular before heading back home to my parking spot between the nandina bushes, unless I saw one of those big blue trucks heading my way up Nineteenth Street. I would vow to stand my ground, poised on the edge of the drive, but it was to no avail. As the blue monster neared with its red ball growing ever more visible, I couldn't help feverishly pedaling myself toward the safety of our carport, safe by a hair, just as it rumbled past the house.

Despite the occasional passing of ominous tractor-trailers, we regularly enjoyed playing in the Fendleys' yard. The sandy loam soil that supported the bushes and shrubs that grew around the house served as a great sandbox, holding a menagerie of buckets and metal dump trucks. Tucked out of the sun behind a lush green cover, it was a perfect spot for hours of play, next to the monkey tree and transplanted Easter lily. The monkey tree was nothing more than some little stumpy tree that had a furry feel to its bark, particularly where new branches spouted forth. But it was our sacred ritual to touch the top of the fuzzy plant whenever we passed by its olive-green stalk, making the day seem a little less common, our street, a little more exotic. And then there was the house itself. The only multi-storied frame structure on the block, it dwarfed the rest of ours. It housed the Fendley brood, which included three or four teenagers "a lot" older than Darren.

As big and intriguing as the two-story was, I saw very little of it. By the time Darren came along, maybe Mrs. Fendley discouraged a herd of children running through her home, or maybe playing in Darren's room would have been frowned upon because I was a girl. We did, however, spend a great deal of time in the family room, where a black and white television stood in the corner with a set of rabbit ears on top that Darren turned from time to time, so we could get a better picture of late-afternoon cartoons. Ricochet Rabbit was one of our favorite characters, most likely due to his holster and gun, much like the cap guns and holsters we wore belted and tied to our thighs. Huckleberry Hound was another favorite, featured alongside his famous friends, Yogi and Boo-Boo Bear. Huckleberry was blue, spoke with a slow Southern drawl and always remained "cool" under heat.

Cartoons were great, but even better were the days when we played in the upstairs hall with the lights turned off, so we could shine the spotlight from atop Darren's huge destroyer battleship into the darkness. The thing rolled on wheels, took up the length of the hall and was deemed sacred; we never took it off the second story. Few and fuzzy memories remain from inside the Fendley house, but I vividly remember some accidents that occurred on the outside in quick succession. The first was the time Darren's cousin dumped some substance into the burning trash, and it blew up in his face. The second was my own mishap.

On a rainy day, Darren and I were racing up the back porch steps that led into the kitchen when I slipped on the wet surface and caught my face on the corner of the top step. I made it inside, where Mrs. Fendley applied a dishtowel to my face to stop the bleeding before calling my mom and loading Darren and me in their enormous boat of a car. It was white just like the color of their house and felt like it could hold the whole neighborhood in the backseat. I sat, traumatized and small, watching the windshield wipers slap against the glass. The next memory is of Mom and Dad cutting one of my favorite t-shirts off me, rather than pulling it over my head, and applying a nice white, pristine bandage to my face. My black eye and hemorrhaged sclera must have impressed the photographer taking my school picture that year. He positioned me in side-profile, but the portrait captured the bruises just the same. Another white-pristine-bandage memory applied to my foot, and the incident most likely occurred that same year.

As customary, I was down the street playing at the Hamptons' house while Mom was at work or running an errand. Joy Hampton was my babysitter when Mom worked part-time at White's auto store downtown. I stayed there in the mornings until Mom came home at lunch, except closer to Christmas, when Mom worked full-time to help out and make some extra Christmas money. The Hamptons were our neighbors and friends as well. Wayne and Joy had three daughters in somewhat stair-step order, each separated by two to three years. Karen, whom I adored, was the oldest and tallest. She was two years older than I was, and I waited impatiently every day for her to come home from school. Julie was the middle golden-haired child, and Laurie was the baby who threw major tantrums upon her rocking horse or in the den chair, rocking each as hard as she could while wailing as loud as she could. Her rocking horse was positioned in the middle of their carport: the slam of the back screen door was followed by her mounting up, rocking and wailing until she played out or went to sleep.

This particular morning, a group of us were sitting on the curb in front of the Hampton house, conversing back and forth with a group of boys on Darren's curb, most likely Robbie and Rex, also good buddies of Darren's who lived directly across from the Fendleys. I decided to run across the street to make my point, without looking, when a car stopped me. Most likely five years old, I distinctly remember the difference between *run over by a car* versus *car stopping on my foot* being pointedly made. The poor old man in his old, old car slowly making his way north on Nineteenth Street didn't have the reflexes to avoid the little girl who didn't look south before darting out in front of him. But he was driving slowly enough and reacted quickly enough to stop and back up over my foot instead of just sitting on top of it. Poor Joy Hampton, running down the driveway in a panic over her babysitting charge sitting on the curb with a crushed foot. After an x-ray and stiff white bandage, everything was okay.

My accident was enough drama for one morning, but *real* accidents spurred tales worth sharing for weeks—like the car wreck that happened on the corner of Nineteenth and Bonham Streets one late summer evening. Two blocks north of my well-pedaled driveway was a busy intersection that I knew very well. My two-story red brick school stood on one corner, facing Mr. Hindman's Phillips 66 gas station on the opposite side of Nineteenth. Hank's burger shop and market faced the Phillips 66 on Bonham Street, and the Texaco service station and Camp Paris trailer park stood opposite Hank's on Nineteenth Street, rounding out the corner across from the school. A stoplight hung over the middle of the intersection.

One evening after dinner while making my tricycle rounds on the driveway, I heard a loud boom but couldn't tell from which direction it came. Then, like in a scene from the *Twilight Zone* (circa 1960s), I looked down my street to witness the whole neighborhood emptying out of their houses with their dinner napkins still in hand or around their necks, moving in family units toward the end of their driveways to stare past me up Nineteenth Street. A car had crashed into the giant pole that held the traffic light and smashed it into the leg of the woman passenger in the front seat, as well. A crowd of onlookers soon began gathering in the schoolyard to get a better look, resembling gatherings that took place for the annual school Halloween carnival. Though I didn't make it down to the corner to see the actual wreckage, I did see the aftermath of the split wooden pole and heard plenty of stories regarding the "meat" coming out of the woman's leg and a dogfight that had to be broken up in the middle of the excited crowd while emergency workers attended to the wreck victims (or, in those days, simply hauled them quickly away in an ambulance). It was a big Saturday night on Nineteenth.

Though it was on the west edge of town, separated from the heart of Paris by a wide expanse of railroad tracks, my street was the center of the world, and I made it a point to be out and around it and its inhabitants every day that weather and circumstances allowed. That long black river of asphalt that ran in front of my house and into the distance farther than I could see must have stood for something more than a crossing at which to look both ways (a point on which I had failed). It was more than a place of accidents where my knees got skinned up enough times to leave scars to this day. It was home for a short while. It was a time and place to return to emotionally as well as physically, and though I stayed away for thirty-eight years, I left a space for it to reside—a void where, on lonely days, only its memory could fill. My memory of summer's hazy days lingering was more palpable than the actual returning.

When stopped by the traffic light still hanging in the middle of the intersection, I sometimes glance down Nineteenth and see the corner street lamp's shining down through the large oak on Austin Street, sending just enough light to make out that slightly curved hollow. A ripple of warmth runs through me as I remember somewhere that is long ago in place of what remains.

Chapter 2
The Best Day of My Life

It's hard to say why, really. Some people have the knack of being happy wherever they are, even classifying their current station in life as the best. I've never been one of those. In fact, when classmates of mine continually pined for increased chronological numbers after their name, I wished for the opposite. I wanted to return to blissful days of early childhood where hours of pretend and play topped the day's agenda, a time when imagination was so real that it could not be explained to or understood by the non-believer. In that time and place, I might conceivably come close to defining my best day.

I can most readily testify to the ones that were definitely not, like the days when Freddy came to play. The older couple living in the pink cinder-block house across Austin Street had grandchildren who would visit periodically. Phyllis and Freddy, though from separate families, were two of those grandchildren who would show up every so often on a Saturday. They almost never visited at the same time. They didn't look the same either. Phyllis was taller and a couple of years older than I was, a big, bossy, black-haired girl with a blunt bob and thick bangs that were always way above her thick black eyebrows. Her darkened face was sprinkled with freckles, but not to the extent of Freddy's.

Freddy was a typical carrot-top, freckled-face boy with as much fire within to match the fiery red atop his head, and he wasn't just sprinkled with freckles; he was covered. I figured this somehow gave him the right or cause to be mean to me. He wasn't as bossy and know-it-all as Phyllis, and he wasn't exactly a bully; he was just sort of mean, mischievous and always seemed to have the upper hand, except once.

We were in my backyard on a Saturday afternoon playing cowboys and Indians, cops and robbers or something that involved a bb gun. I was the one being hunted, and we met at the pink-bricked, blind back corner of my house.

It was scary enough coming face-to-face with his beady little eyes as we peered around from opposite ends of the corner, but the fact that he held his bb gun cocked and ready to fire didn't help matters either. Without thinking (or so he said), he discharged a bb into my neck. I had been shot! He dropped his gun, put his arm around my shoulder and begged and pleaded for me to stop crying and not tell anybody. "I'll buy you candy, anything you want, if you just won't tell on me." Either his desperate pleas or his promise of candy made an impression on me, because I never told anyone, even though I never got any candy.

Many, many years later while working in a pediatric intensive care unit during my pediatric residency, I was assigned to follow a patient returning from neurosurgery following the removal of a bb that had penetrated his *Tentorium cerebelli*. (Latin for "tent of the cerebellum," it is an anatomic structure in the brain that is an extension of the outer membrane that covers the brain and spinal cord, separating the cerebellum from the inferior portion of the occipital lobes of the brain). Here's some kid returning from surgery with a white bandage on his head escorted by the neurosurgical team, while I'm thinking, *I got shot with a bb once. Maybe the thing is still in my neck and one day will silently erode through my carotid artery causing a sudden inexplicable death. Thanks, Freddy.*

As mean as Freddy was, his legacy fades in comparison to another little boy who showed up periodically to play on our street. His name was Jerry. Jerry's mother, Freda, came to have coffee and visit occasionally with my morning babysitter, Joy Hampton. During a time when many mothers stayed home raising children and helped other mothers who worked or had appointments or errands to run, morning coffee breaks while the kids played outside were typical. But mornings with Freda and Jerry were anything but typical. Freda was a lovely woman with stylish short hair and a warm smile. She was soft-spoken, sophisticated, and had the patience of Job. Jerry was the brewing volcano that erupts without warning, the pot of boiling water that suddenly hisses and foams over the top, the out-of-the-blue dog bite or bee sting—in other words, a catastrophe looking for a place to happen. When Jerry came to play, a trail of crying, injured kids leading in and out of the Hampton house would finally accumulate into *the last straw* that could no longer be ignored. It would prompt an end to the coffee break and a quick exit with Jerry, depriving his mom from any further respite from him.

One morning with Jerry, remembered without passion, went something like this. In a game of chase in the backyard and around the house, I looked back while running, to see Julie (the middle Hampton child) thrown to the ground and trampled, her blanket still clutched tightly in her small hand. While enjoying a game on their beautiful bricked-in patio, I see Jerry take the youngest Hampton girl, Laurie, by the hair, and slam her head into the brick wall without provocation. Engaged in a game of cowboys and Indians, or some kind of play, again involving guns and revolvers, Jerry hits Trey, another backyard neighbor, in the head with a metal toy pistol. BAM! This time, however, Trey's momma intervenes from the other side of the ravine. She comes out her sliding-glass back door and tells Trey to go over and hit that boy as hard as he can. Little Trey approaches Jerry to carry out the punishment, and Jerry falls apart to such extent that his howls mortify Trey. He can barely bring himself to tap Jerry on the arm, much less hit him with his own gun... And then, finally, the straw that breaks the camel's back, the event that finally relieves us of Jerry for a while.

We are all sitting in chairs lined up in rows in the Hampton's carport, waiting for a club meeting or some kind of program to start: very important stuff. The sun is out, all is right in the world of make-believe and magic, except I'm seated next to Jerry. Seated in Laurie's bright pink rocking chair, I'm eye level with Jerry who is a couple of years younger than me. He turns to look me in the eye, and, without uttering a word, slaps my face so hard it draws blood. Holding a wet rag to my face and drawing in gulps of air between my heaving sobs, I was vaguely aware of Freda's smiling face and gentle wave as she reluctantly but hurriedly bid her hostess goodbye, while whisking Jerry to the car.

It was always said that Jerry was an only child and didn't know how to play with other kids, but years of pediatric training brings Jerry's direct but sometimes vacant stare and impulsive behavior into sharp focus. Jerry probably fit somewhere on the spectrum of autism, a child with "pervasive developmental disorder not otherwise specified," terms unknown and certainly not understood back then within the context of a kid who just couldn't play well with other kids.

Other days, of course, were good days because of the people who were there to share them. Dickey was the most beautiful boy I had ever seen. He was the grandson of Mrs. Wilson who lived next door. Though she had other grandsons—three, in fact, who lived just outside of town—Dickey was the only one I played with, and he came too seldom. From time to time, he traveled up from South Texas with his mother, Ruby. She was a tall, statuesque brunette with natural curls and red lipstick. He was older than I was by a couple or more years. I was mesmerized by the way the light played with his hair and shone through his blue eyes. His nickname was Dickey-bird, or that's what my brother always called him, though I never knew why. Days with Dickey that happened long ago were simple, but they were special enough that time did not let me forget them, or him: like the time we took black markers and drew faces on the indigenous orange day lilies that grew by the edge of the wood. I was too young to draw, but the face of a lady on a lily, placed there by my older friend, made such an impression on me I never looked at orange lilies the same. The day we built a clubhouse in the back of Carol's backyard was a pretty big deal too.

Carol was closer in age to Dickey, maybe even a year or two older, and she lived on Austin Street next door to Freddy's grandparents. She was the youngest in her family; most of her siblings were grown and gone, except for Sue, who occasionally lived there with her husband and small daughter. I loved Carol. Dark headed, sporting a "flip" hairstyle and cat-eye glasses, she was always good to me and let me come over as often as I pleased to sit on her front porch swing and tag along with her older girlfriends. We spent a sunny Saturday afternoon during one of Dickey's visits, converting an old lawnmower shed attached to her dad's garage into our clubhouse. I certainly couldn't read the red-painted letters on the sign we tacked up on the shed, but the sign held memories of Dickey whenever I saw it, even as the rain and time faded its red away. But another Saturday with Dickey came along unexpectedly and still stands on its own as "a good day."

The Disney musical, *Mary Poppins*, debuted in 1964 and showed up at the Grand Theatre, downtown Paris, Texas, sometime that summer. Apparently, Ruth had arranged with my mother for me to go with Dickey and his mother to the afternoon show. It was my first time to go inside the movie theater, and I was driven there in true fashion, sitting on the huge backseat of Ruth's new white Chevy Impala, with white vinyl seats striped in red, the same shade as Ruth's lipstick. Now I had never heard of Julie Andrews, though she was a star in her own right after wowing fans on Broadway as Liza Doolittle in *My Fair Lady,* but I readily recognized Dick Van Dyke. I had seen him trip over that ottoman in his front living room numerous times while watching *The Dick Van Dyke Show* during morning re-runs and prime-time television. Even so, I was mesmerized by Mrs. Andrews and the children in the movie and didn't really appreciate the intertwining roles of Dick Van Dyke's chimney sweep and the aloof father in the story, Mr. Banks, until years later.

Greeted by the bright afternoon sun that blinded us after stepping out of the blackened theater, I suddenly felt the little town where I lived and I had both changed within the time it had taken to watch the movie. For one thing, the downtown First United Methodist Church and its red-tiled dome held a strange new resemblance to the cathedral featured in the movie. From that time on, I began to picture the Bird Woman, played by Jane Darwell, sitting on the church's tall front steps with her bags of seed calling for us to "Feed the Birds," supremely sung by Julie Andrews. The music, in my head and in every other school-age child around, penetrated our homes, games and bedtime prayers.

In a time when the only ways to experience a movie again were a return to the theater (most unlikely) or a two-part special featured presentation on the Sunday night *Walt Disney's World of Color,* we were relegated to listening to 45s and the album of the *Mary Poppins* soundtrack that played on our parents' hi-fi's or, in my case, a Phonola record player. I danced and sang to that album for years. Just hearing the opening bars of the overture helped me relive that afternoon: Dickey and I, and my first picture show in a movie theater once studded with a hundred light bulbs that hung from the outside marquee. That was a good day.

Dickey only came around every so often, but I had a friend directly across Nineteenth Street whom I could see daily, provided I looked both ways before running over to the Aylor household. Gwen Aylor, the only girl in a family of four teenagers, knew me before I ever knew her, but I considered her a friend as well as babysitter and mentor, and I didn't feel the least bit intimidated about making myself at home in her house, especially the Aylors' kitchen. If it perturbed her to have me waltz in every day to sit on her bed and watch her get ready or ask her a million questions, she never let me know. In fact, she acted quite the opposite; Gwen spoiled me right along with the rest of her family. Maybe it was the fact that the family dog, Joe, loved me dearly and followed me everywhere I went, or the fact that her parents, Jim and Ruth, considered me their first unofficial grandchild, or that I was just two months old when we moved in across the street. Whatever the reason, she welcomed me, entertained me with her 45s, and never ran me off. I adored her.

Gwen introduced me to the teenage years of the mid-1960s more so than my own brother, who was in the same grade as Gwen. The bohemian subculture that was brewing in Haight Ashbury had not taken roots in Paris, Texas; one was still likely to hear Brenda Lee on the radio while attempting dances introduced and sung by Chubby Checker. Rhythm and Blues, surf rock and Doo Wop were still musical mainstays, although no one could resist the British Invasion and naming their favorite Beatle. Gwen was in the thick of it with her short, pixie-style haircut with a bouffant crown, teased and sprayed. She was fun and outgoing, involved in school stuff, and held her own, living with three brothers who seemed to adore her as well. She talked on the phone with her girlfriends, dated and did typical teenage-girl stuff, but also let me tag along with both eyes wide open witnessing changes in her (e.g., having her ears' pierced by our neighbor, Willie Ray Morgan, with nothing but ice, an ice pick, and cork a couple of hours before her Saturday night date) that signaled things to come: graduation, college, marriage and so forth.

Changes came for both of us, but I didn't think they would come so quickly for me. Things were different at the Aylor household after Gwen graduated from Paris High School, along with my brother, with whom she attended prom. (They both must have been between steadies, because they had known each other since they were twelve years old and acted more like brother and sister.) Gwen attended the local junior college and was more intent on having the books out, spread all over the dining room table, than spending hours with me in her room or cruising downtown. We no longer sat on the front porch, where she had tried to teach me (unsuccessfully) how to whistle or (successfully) how to blow bubblegum bubbles. Even the dog seemed to take notice; he relentlessly followed me around, sometimes right up to the school's front door before being told to go back home. My brother went off to Air Force basic training, because my dad was afraid of the draft and told him to pick an armed service and join rather than wait for Uncle Sam to call. Since the teenagers across both sides of Nineteenth Street began to disappear and go on to other things, there seemed to be little reason for me to visit the Aylor household, announced or unannounced. Even Robert, the youngest of the Aylors, seemed too preoccupied while sitting in front of the television, and, for the first time, I began to feel somewhat like a stranger going out the Aylors' front door, kind of awkward and unsure of my return. I would soon learn that the feeling of change was a foreshadowing of things to come.

One fall day, after walking the two blocks from school, I arrived home to find a strange yellow sign on a black metal stand staked in front of our large oak tree: House for Sale. I love the way my parents prepared me, nothing like a shocker instead of cookies and milk after school. My dad had been transferred with his company, and we were moving to a town an hour's drive to the west. It was a larger distance than it sounds or even sounded at the time. Just a few months after my startling discovery, we left the corner of Nineteenth and Austin, as well as my old school and all I had known. While mom drove us away, I sat in the front seat, staring out the passenger window at the familiar houses, school, even the Texaco station and Bud's Market flashing past me. As we drove down Bonham Street heading west, a school friend of mine was half-walking, half-skipping along the sidewalk on her way home from school, oblivious to the passing cars and February's gray skies. I didn't act fast enough to get the window down in time for a final wave or goodbye; I could only stare back at her fading figure in the rearview window as we left Paris behind.

I didn't see Gwen the day we left, but I did see Ruth, her mom, and Joe. Joe was as hard for me to leave as if he'd been my own. We had become close over the past year, even though he had been around since I was a baby. Ruth came over to see us off while the moving van was loading up and brought us gifts. Mine was a beautiful new dress with a lace overlay on the bodice, a pink skirt and a wide sash that tied in a large bow that hung down my back. I proudly wore it for picture day at my new school. It would be at least a year or two before Mom and I returned to Paris for a visit. Joe lay in the flower bed outside the garage by the Aylor back door and hardly raised his head to greet me. He had forgotten me. Mom and Ruth visited while I sat on the front porch, watching a group of boys come down the street wearing baseball caps and fiddling with a ball. I was too shy to call out to see if they were my old friends Darren, Robbie and Rex. They whispered among themselves as they looked my direction but kept walking. I can't remember if I saw Gwen that day, but I fondly remember seeing her the next time we visited Paris, a summer or two later.

Gwen was married one June afternoon in the small intimate chapel on the local junior college campus. I traveled with Mom and Dad the hour's drive east for the event, all of us dressed in our Sunday best, with me in the back seat, relishing the familiar sites upon returning. Ruth came down the aisle in her typical animated manner, stopping to greet and wave to people as she made her way down to the front pew. Gwen was escorted down the aisle by her father, Jim. She wore a knee-length white dress with a lace overlay, white pumps and small white veil that covered her eyes and hung down the back of her neck, covering her pixie-style cut with the little poof on top. Although the event was simple, a woman in a deep fuchsia-colored dress stepped forth in the small balcony at the front of the chapel and elegantly sang one of the most beautiful renditions of The Lord's Prayer I have ever heard since the summer of my tenth year.

After the wedding, we all adjourned to the banquet room of the local Holiday Inn for the reception, where I stood taking in the sights of her three brothers who were older than I remembered, two of them married and moved on. Gwen left us waving in the parking lot as her new dark-haired husband drove the two of them off in their custom-designed car covered in shaving cream and shoe polish, trailing ribbons of coke cans—compliments of the bride's younger brother, Robert. It was the last time I would see her.

Gwen moved to the Dallas area with her husband where they worked and raised a family. She taught at an elementary school and had a little dark-haired boy who was the spitting image of his father. Gwen was diagnosed with uterine cancer several years after the birth of her son and died while he was still very young—younger than the school-age children she had taught until she was no longer able. Her young class sat together at her funeral. I was in high school at the time and did not attend the out-of-town funeral with my parents. Only one other "old neighbor" from Paris attended the funeral as well; he was an aging taxi driver who had once delivered a young Gwen to and from her dance classes held in the downtown Gibraltar Hotel. Upon returning home from school that day, I found my dad sitting in our den, somewhat shell-shocked from the service. He said he thought he would never get away from Ruth, who clung to him, sobbing, after thanking my parents for coming to the funeral. I was somewhat sorry I hadn't gone to the service, sorry I didn't get the chance to see the family, or her little boy for the first time, sorry I hadn't kept up with her, for it may have been Gwen who gave me one of the best days of my life.

• • • •

It was a sun-filled Saturday. Saturdays trumped all days of the week as far as I was concerned: no school, no church, nothing to get up for except morning cartoons. The afternoon was filled with hours playing down the block or time spent walking around the downtown square with my mom, in and out of the shops. The day ended with television—especially if the Saturday night movie featured Elvis Presley. After dinner, my TV viewing began with *The Lawrence Welk Show*. That's right: I was a huge fan of the eloquent-spoken band director with the slender white baton and bubbles on the dance floor as he waltzed the "blue-hairs" from the audience around a turn or two. I loved watching Jo Ann Castle tear up the piano, Arthur Duncan tap his little feet like crazy, Bobby waltz with his childhood partner, Barbara Boylan, and listening to the Lennon Sisters—I loved all four of them. But sunny, lazy Saturday afternoons were the best, and on one such day, I found myself in Gwen's bedroom feeling quite pampered and royal-like.

Gwen's bedroom was at the front of the Aylor house and looked out on Nineteenth Street. It was bigger than the middle bedroom where the three Aylor teen boys slept on twin beds, including one set of bunk beds. But then, they had a door that came off their room to the outside where they kept their car parked alongside the house, for convenience sake, I'm sure. As much as I liked playing on the bunk beds, the boys' room was nothing compared to Gwen's; it was magical. Her bed held a matching set of pickaninny dolls, one male and female, dressed in white shirts with red polka-dot patterned pants and dress, respectfully. The momma doll wore gold earrings. Above Gwen's bed and on her walls hung ballerina prints in pastels featuring male and female dancers in graceful poses. Their plastic French provincial frames were a thing of beauty. Her dresser held teenage-girl paraphernalia as well as her closet and bedside table, but the best stuff sat on the floor in front of her window: her record player with a gold, spiraled record rack that held her 45s and my personal favorite.

Before the Beatles' breakout, the most popular rock and pop band in America was the Four Seasons. In 1962 they came out with their first album entitled *Sherry,* which was also the title of their first number-one hit song (spelled correctly, I might add). The song took on the nickname, "Sherry Baby," which was in the lyrics and was appropriately attached to me as well. It was a huge hit in my house and neighborhood, and Gwen played it to such an extent that my brother grew sick and tired of it, but the term stuck with me. On this particular Saturday, Gwen had "Sherry Baby" cranked while I sat before her, after dancing my own rendition of "The Twist." She patiently applied great effort to get a brush through my hair, and, after what seemed like hours, managed to get my hair into a ponytail held by an elastic band with colorful balls interlacing each other. My father was so proud of the effect—or maybe he just appreciated how proud I was of my new "do"—that he took a picture of me astride Joe in our front yard.

There we sit—the old rogue who followed me to school and whom I had to leave behind eventually, bathed in the glow of the afternoon's sunlight, on pretty much a perfect day.

Chapter 3
Burl and Opal

At two distinct times, a golden haze creates a lazy stillness over the countryside. One such time is in the early afternoon, shortly after the noon meal, and the other is on Sunday evening, an hour or so before sundown. I know it when I see it. When I'm in that moment, it's the same as it was—but I experience it less frequently now. These days I find it at the end of the bike trail that runs through our town of about 26,000. One day, fund-raising efforts will extend the black asphalt trail, linking pedestrians and cyclists moving west and east.

Built on a reclaimed railroad track, the trail comes to a dead end in the next little neighboring community, where the pasture lands begin on either side of the track. On the south side of the track, grasslands dotted with cows and barbed-wire fences run unimpeded toward the distant horizon. Here at the end of the day I pause and look over the land, reminiscing about a time that has passed as a way of life for some, but, in particular, a time that held a place and people I can no longer find. The house is no longer standing at the end of a white-rock drive, and they have passed on now, many years, but I have an obsession to see the cows grazing in these unknown fields before I can pedal my bicycle back home. Although these are not my granddad's cows, I have connected cows to his memory since I was very small. When reciting the "little piggy" rhymes while pulling at our own "little piggies," I grew up faithfully reciting the third line, "This little piggy had *Granddaddy's* roast beef." And though I see no resemblance in these cows to the small herds he ran, that same golden haze hanging over the land puts me right back in the side yard of that old farm house, as if I were still small enough to come out from hiding under the yellow jasmine bush in time for dinner.

If his legacy is his love for the cows and land and all he did to keep them in shape, it would only be somewhat overshadowed by the care and fuss of his mate. My granny oversaw a true gardener's garden, but she made sure things grew all around the place. Never trying for a landscaped, picturesque yard and home, she simply liked to make pretty things grow—along the walk, by the porch, or trellising up a handmade wooden frame. She was a large and practical woman. She had a purpose; her garden had a purpose. Even so, she did it all with a song, whether it was putting food on the table or making clothes or quilts to go on the bed. Her work was her praise, and, though the garden yielded fresh food and enough left over to fill her deep freeze throughout the year, it was always bordered by flowers, a testament to how much joy her work brought her. It was just the way she was, and for good reason. Though they were together for sixty years in the truest sense, they couldn't be more different in temperament and physicality.

"Here comes the bride, big fat and wide; Here comes the groom, skinny as a broom," we sang with all our might, while she laughed right along with her three granddaughters. They were true to the rhyme: she was always overweight and found it difficult to push away from the table (though she faithfully dropped saccharin in her iced tea or drank Tab), and he was small and wiry. She was content to tend to her home and garden, the things that needed to be done routinely: cooking, washing, mending, hoeing, while he raced out the door to drive his pickup to and from the fields, feeding cows, checking the mail, running to the store, checking the water pump, going to the sale barn. She was as jovial and fun-loving as she was big; he was impatient and a bit ornery. She was anxious and wrung her hands over the silliest things; he would lose his temper over the littlest things. They complimented each other like Barney Fife and Aunt Bea: one, impulsive and bursting with restless energy; the other, often over-nurturing and incapable of getting riled up over his demands and fast pace. By the time I knew her, it was like "water off a duck's back." "Any tea?" he was known for asking repeatedly over the years, seated at the dinner table, impatiently shaking his emptied glass. Of course there was tea. There was always tea, sweet tea in the ceramic pitcher every day of their lives together (and he knew it).

Burl Lee Shields was born June 19, 1904, the second oldest of seven children. Opal Hunter followed a year later, born November 2, 1905, to L. C. and Susie Hunter, the youngest of nine children and the only redhead in the bunch. I say followed, because they were both born and raised in the same rural community of Sedalia, Texas (a little northeast of Dallas), which can no longer be found on a map. Sedalia's one-room school taught and housed them both and provided them with the lifelong friendship of their teacher and mentor, Mrs. Jernigan. As early as four years of age, Opal played with a boy in the schoolyard named Burl. It was a time of horse and buggy, mule and wagon or simply walking along dirt roads with lunch pail in hand. Grades one through eight stood straight and tall, stacked on risers by the side of the schoolhouse for picture day. If you had shoes, you wore them; if you didn't, you came and stood for the picture just the same. Most of the boys looked like they had just come from the fields or would return there after school. The same could be said for the roughened look of the girls, excusing the fact that they were not wearing striped bib overalls.

My great-grandfather must have approved of Burl at one time, for he warned my granny of "jumping over a little flower into a cow pile," while contemplating her affections for another boy. She once told me that, years later, when her father started to make some complaint over my granddad's ways, she swiftly countered with, "You'd better watch what you say, that's your little flower you wanted." He must have approved of the wedding, because it was assumed they would be returning to her parents' home to spend the night after the ceremony. It was a simple affair, very simple. On a summer afternoon in 1924, the young couple pulled up in front of the preacher's house in Westminster, Texas (which can no longer be found on a map, either). He came out with Bible in hand to greet the pair sitting in an open car. He pronounced them man and wife right where they sat, before watching them drive off to spend nearly sixty years together.

The first ornery act on the part of my granddad was to take his new wife over to his cousin Clem's house to stay the night.

"Well, that's just not right," my granny told me. "You need to tell somebody if you're going to stay somewhere else. Everybody was expecting us to come back home." (The whole thing sounded "not right" to me, married while sitting in a car and staying with kinfolk afterward—parents or cousins.)

They were rural people; they continued living in and around the small community of Sedalia. In fact, my granny never lived more than fifteen miles from her birthplace during her married adult years, excluding the last decade or so of her life, spent in a health care facility. They did what most others around them did during that time: lived off the land and tried to accrue a little money to buy a place of their own someday. They farmed, grew and picked cotton alongside extended family that lived nearby on the same blackland. Throughout his life my granddad farmed but held other jobs to supplement the income as well. For a short time in the mid-1930s, they owned a small country store in the community. They sold it to a cousin in the latter part of the decade, then bought it back around 1941 and ran it through World War II when goods such as coffee, sugar, cigarettes and gasoline had to be rationed. It was the hub of their small farming community, and many folks came to the store to get "news" about the outside world from the flour, grocery and candy salesmen, as well as the gasoline truck drivers. They traded it for a farm in 1949, and it later burned to the ground in the mid-'50s. Burl worked for a time at the local air force base, worked the entrance gate at an IBM plant and drove a school bus for many years while Opal tended to house, garden, farm and animals. It wasn't so much about what they did, but who they were and how they did what they did.

As different as they were, they had many parallel traits and associations. For one, they were both liked, extremely liked by family and friends. They were fun in their own unique way. He was quick, impulsive and had a way with kids, loved the grandkids, loved being with the grandkids. He loved visiting and talking with others, wanted to be in the thick of things and was a yellow-dog Democrat. He was elected to two terms as mayor of the small hamlet of Tom Bean, Texas. Unbeknownst to my granny, she first heard of my granddad's new appointment when women from the church began to congratulate her one morning outside the Sunday school classroom. Later that day, while sitting in their den chairs she turned and asked, "Daddy, are you the mayor?"

"Yep," he replied, hastily reaching for his hat and keys, on his way out to the pickup truck. Time to go to the barn.

While he always seemed to be in an impatient hurry, she hummed and sang throughout her day. She somehow always made time for the grandkids in the middle of cooking, watering the livestock, weeding the garden, etc. She didn't stop for us; she simply tolerated us weaving in and out around her and the tasks that never seemed to end. She made us laugh as well as made herself laugh, often at the expense of making fun of herself and allowing us to do the same. And as clueless and tolerant as she seemed with Granddad's remarks and ways, she would surprise us every once in a while with her learned sense of humor. Once, we passed my granny (humming, as usual) at the kitchen sink while on our way out the back door to gather some corn just harvested from a neighboring farm. She called over her shoulder, "You'd better take some sacks with you." In a huff, my granddad replied, "Naw, I thought we'd carry all fifty pounds by hand." "Oh, your arms might get tired if you do that," she sing-songed back. With a snort, he swept out the door. I'm sure she kept right on humming, finishing the dishes before happily starting supper.

 Associations: I cannot look at a pack of M&M's without thinking of my granddad. He used to throw them to my younger cousin from the school bus window when he passed her house on his afternoon route. A ride in the back of his pickup meant candy and a bottle of pop for sure. When he headed out the door on his way to the store for milk and bread, my cousins and I made sure we were already seated over the tire hubs in the back of the truck. My cousin Diana thinks her younger sister, Karen, was treated more than any of us, but my brother readily points out, "Nope, I was around twelve years before any of you guys." He bought us treats, she made them for us. Even if we had the recipes, we could not replicate the taste of her caramel-iced cake, banana pudding, cherry pies, and others. Her kitchen continually smelled of butter and vanilla, like they were infused into the cabinetry, dishes and walls. And she did not skimp on the sugar or any other ingredient, if it called for two cups, that's what you got. "Lite" and sugar-free were not in her vocabulary, except for the saccharin bottle that stood next to the salt and pepper shakers at every meal.

 He took care of the cows; she took care of the chickens, and in more ways than one. She raised them from chicks that arrived via post every spring. She fed, watered and gathered the eggs, but, come time for dinner (in the country, dinner is typically the noon meal), one of them had their neck wrung and was served up nice and fried within an hour's time. He tinkered with tractors, plows and gadgets on the farm; she kept that old black Singer humming by pumping its large foot treadle while running a seam. At the time of her death, very few store-bought dresses hung in her closet, and she never owned or sewed on anything electric. He sang in the choir with all his might (though according to tale, he couldn't hold a pitch); she attended the ladies Sunday school class. He brought home the bacon; she cooked it. He slept on the left; she slept on the right. He drove; she rode, except an occasional run to the store and when he needed some help with the farming equipment.

One vivid summer day, I stood in the hot sun and dust next to some field my granddad was helping combine. It was shortly after noon and for some reason Granny and I had come out to where he and another man were working, possibly to bring them lunch. I don't fully recall the circumstances, but he asked her to back up the combine while he directed her to where he needed it placed. She was up in the cab, backing it out, alright, clear into the ditch, with his running alongside, banging on the side of the large machine trying to get her attention and make her stop before it was too late. There it rested, in the hot sun, down in a ditch. To this day I don't know how they got it out. It seemed catastrophic to me at the time, particularly when I saw my granddad, first in sprint mode, then in his usual exasperation mode at the inability of her to hear him and do something just exactly the way he wanted it done. Granny and I just went home in the pickup truck, with me puzzling over the turn of events, which didn't seem to faze her all that much. At least we were in the pickup and not out by the rows of grain, scratching our heads and wondering whom to call to help us out of such a predicament. The pickup was, after all, the most special place to be while visiting the grandparents, just edging out a ride on the tractor and climbing into the hayloft. On that, my cousins and even my brother would agree.

The make was a 1964 Chevrolet pickup, though it always seemed older, probably because it saw more off-road adventures than most modern all-terrain vehicles today. I have never since seen the color: some mauve-tan, milk-toast shade best described as the color of a piece of Dubble Bubble gum that had been thoroughly chewed, spit out on the sidewalk, and after a few days picked up on the bottom of a leather-soled shoe. It had an AM radio that I don't ever recall hearing, a heater used only in the bitter cold, an oil light that was always on, hole in the floorboard, shifter on the column and the best bed that ever shuffled granddaughters to and from the general store. I'm convinced that there is no other place that M&M's and Nehi soft drinks (no matter the flavor) can be enjoyed to the extent we did while the wind blew our hair and plastered it against our sticky faces riding in the back of that pickup.

There never seemed to be any concern with gas or how far and to where the pickup would take us. It herded cattle, carried stacks of baled hay, took us to and from the pasture, the store, carried my brother and the horse trailer to rodeos, and got us to church without fail. And though it was clearly Granddad's truck, he was not above sharing; in fact, he insisted on it. He had me behind the wheel around age ten years, and my brother, possibly even younger, because he was always obsessed with driving. After fastening the gate to the cow pasture, a loop of wire that slipped over the bois d'arc tree post, my granddad would slide over to the passenger side and let me get in behind the wheel. This became a ritual after feeding the cows as often as I came to visit, and sometimes our rides extended into the countryside where I learned to honk the horn as I rounded a "blind corner" on some narrow back road. Most of the time I drove, and he shifted, stretching his legs over to work the clutch and gas, but he even let me try that a couple of times as well. Steering, shifting and applying the clutch in sync proved a little too challenging while attempting the last turn headed for home. I never seemed to navigate that right-hand turn crisply enough for my granddad, who always assumed I was aiming for the deep culverts on either side, considering the way he shot over to my side of the truck and grabbed the wheel. Years later, willing the car my daughter was driving to avoid hitting the car in front of us by placing my feet against the front floorboard, I recalled his quick, terrified movements and completely concurred.

It was a simpler time, a little more rustic than what I was accustomed to at home, but we never seemed to mind. In fact, I relished farm life to the extent I lay full claim on being raised there, though, actually, my time there only comprised disconnected visits and occasional extended stays. But few memories have pervaded and remained so intact, down to the smallest of details, as those of my grandparents' farm houses and surroundings. Some things changed, most things are now gone, but much remains almost palpable by simple recall.

It was a full step down into the only bathroom in the house, just off the den, or the room where the television and Granddad's swivel chair resided. Behind the curtained shelf on the left were the towels; a white, rickety toilet to your immediate right; white sink on the opposite wall with a mirrored medicine cabinet that hung above it; and a white bathtub at the end, surrounded by fake tile board halfway up the wall. No fluff, no fuss, but you could count on a few things: a bar of Lava soap that could scrub off anything, including the top layer of epidermal skin; rough, white-only Scott toilet paper; and a glass bottle of Prell shampoo perched on the edge of the tub. In the early 1960s a classic commercial demonstrated the viscous property of the shampoo: a pearl was dropped into the thick, green liquid, and its slow descent through the emerald sludge was compared favorably to how swiftly the pearl floated effortlessly to the bottom of the "other leading-brand shampoo" (most likely Breck). You were expected to put this thick, green gunk on your head to wash away *whatever* while reveling in its rich lather. God help you if it ever got in your eyes. It burned as bad as the small vial of Merthiolate housed on the second shelf of the medicine cabinet. You had to be one tough customer to enter that bathroom.

It was a sad day for us kids when my grandparents moved from the farm outside of Tom Bean to live inside the "city" limits of Tom Bean, population 500. They went from an old, two-story farmhouse to a one-story, and ninety-plus acres to one—taken up mostly by Granny's garden—and from living at the end of a white-rock drive to sitting on the corner of graveled streets that were eventually paved. I actually knew them longer while they lived in town, but it's hard to disassociate them from our bohemian days of play and mischief along the creek. And if we thought leaving the farm was hard for us, watching them part from each other was even harder.

Oh, we all saw it coming: the frailty, slow to recover from setbacks, losing his way on downtown streets he had walked on since a kid, even failing momentarily to recognize "his own," but we didn't think it would be with such vengeance, so quickly, or maybe we just thought it would never happen. My granddad never recovered after surgery for colon cancer. Bright red blood spotted in the toilet one morning, which he promptly reported to my grandmother, started him and the rest of us on a shortened journey for which we weren't prepared. During a slow, disoriented recovery in the hospital, doctors discovered he had suffered a stroke while under anesthesia; his inability to protect his trachea from food particles would lead to his demise. The last memory I have of him lucid is a vision of him sitting ramrod straight in a high-back chair wearing his white hospital gown, utensils in hand, waiting for his dinner. "Where's the dishes?" he half demanded, half asked my grandmother, as my dad hurriedly escorted out of the room an aide holding a hospital food tray. A nasogastric tube was placed to transport a nutritious goo into his stomach, and he was transferred to the only extended-care facility in the area that was equipped to deal with tube feedings. It was a "nursing home" as far as the rest of us were concerned, the kind of place we frequented on Sunday afternoons, visiting family members who would precede us in death.

It was a short-lived week. The last time I saw him alive, I was directed to "that new patient's room," where not even the name of a once-proud mayor of Tom Bean, Texas, was posted on the patient name plate outside the door. He lay still and sleeping with his nasogastric tube in place, but he did recognize me upon awakening. He gave me that big Jimmy Durante smile, took my hand and wept silently, before talking out of his head and drifting off. While sitting on the side of his bed, I tossed up some kind of poor, pitiful, last-ditch-effort prayer for something I did not even know what to ask for, before silently walking out the door. The next time I saw him, I was standing outside the emergency room door in my white hospital laboratory coat. Notified by my family that he was en route from the nursing home to the hospital, I hurried over from my job in the hospital's pathology lab to greet him. I stood poised outside his door, gazing fondly on the little withered shape of my grandfather as the nurses and technicians attending to him passed in and out of the room. I gingerly inquired if that was Mr. Shields, to which the emergency room doctor re-entering the room responded matter-of-factly, "Yes, he's dead." Stopped by my gasp, she quickly realized the patient was something more to me than just another needle-stick. I must have been waiting for another glimpse of recognition from him; instead, I think some part of that prayer I didn't understand at the time was answered. Once it was apparent he would never be the same, that impulsive spirit that had him jumping in and out of his pickup truck didn't let him lay long in a bed with his hands tied so he couldn't pull out his feeding tube. The same could not be said for Granny.

From the time I was a small child, I remember Granny's fears were never rooted in dying but in surviving past her body's and mind's capabilities. As children, my cousins and I proudly stated our goal of growing to reach one hundred years, to which my granny would reply, in her Northeast Texas accent, "Oh, me, I don't *wont* to live to be a hundred," and, as young as we were, we fully understood her to be certain on that point. When making our visitation rounds through the nursing homes that housed distant family and old friends, it would pain her so to see someone she once knew in an incapacitated state: "Why that's Nell so-and-so! I went to school with that girl," she'd marvel, shaking her head, getting right down in the woman's face, trying to converse with her to see what she needed. If Granny had had her own way, she would have force-fed her oldest sister chocolates just to keep her alive instead of submitting to her futile state of dementia, but sadly the same fate awaited her. The very thing she feared most played itself out over a fourteen-year span in an assisted-living facility in which the hall outside her room became a long country road with suspect neighbors living just across the way.

Now my dad did the best he could. After her increasing agitation and aggression made it apparent that she couldn't continue living with my parents and/or my uncle's family, she was admitted to a long-care facility just down the road from my parents' home. Dad took her ice cream daily and initially visited her twice a day or however many times it took to settle her down. In fact, throughout the years, vacations and trips to visit the grandkids were constructed and shortened to accommodate her: "Gotta get back and see about Granny." She took issue with my dad over things she couldn't understand regarding her new surroundings and strange neighbors: "Vinson [my father] said I couldn't have any scissors. Well, there's not a human in town that doesn't own a pair of scissors!" Well-spoken from someone who sewed all her life and probably once carried a pair around in her dress pockets.

She would eventually befriend the "little girl across the road" (a ninety-plus-year-old woman on her hall), whom she would sit or walk hand in hand with, until she died years before my granny. The years tolled on and—without someone to take care of, like the "little girl"—trips to the beauty shop and cafeteria eventually ceased. Her bed became her home. Unlike my granddad, whose frail frame assisted him with an abrupt exodus, Granny's stalwart frame kept her around long after her mind and senses had left. In fact, that heart kept beating weeks longer than predicted by the consulting hospice team after my dad had made a very difficult decision.

My dad has always said placing his father in a nursing home was harder on him emotionally than grieving over his death. He remains, to this day, torn over my grandmother's death. Upon her admission into a long-term care facility, the managing staff made my father aware that once patients in residence were unable to take in their nutrition orally, feeding tubes would be required for patients to remain in their care. The fact that Granny remained so long in their long-term care actually facilitated her feeding tube placement when she reached end-stage dementia, because no one (including her physician or managing staff) bothered to counsel my father on the change in their stance on feeding tube requirements. Thanks to aggressive lobbying for end-of-life rights, the option for palliative care and hospice in extended care health facilities offered a different approach to addressing end-stage entities rather than applying the standard invasive medical procedures that prolonged the patient's suffering. *This* was not communicated to my father, at all.

After six months of daily watching her skin bruise and peel off due to its thin parchment-like consistency every time she was turned, he had had enough and approached me one day about a decision he was grappling with over her feeding tube. My plan (unbeknownst to him) had worked. I had been working within a pediatric palliative care program for about six months when I asked my parents to accompany me (as babysitters) to a conference I was going to attend with my boss, who would be lecturing on initiating palliative care into mainstream medicine. I had hoped an opportunity would arise for my dad and Dr. Kane to discuss my grandmother's prognosis and condition, allowing Dr. Kane to expound on palliative medicine's goals-of-care pertaining to the patient with end-stage disease and poor quality of life. I believe that by being in an environment targeting these issues something clicked with Dad that caused him to rethink this decision. "I'm going to have to hold my mother's hand and watch her die," he shakily stated, to which I replied, "She's dying now, Dad, but by continuing the g-tube feedings we are extending the dying process and prolonging her suffering."

I had to hand it to him, when he made up his mind to do the best thing, the most loving thing for my grandmother, he never backed down. A day or so after signing for removal of the g-tube and a hospice consult, he called me: "She hasn't looked this good in years." Hospice had provided a new air mattress and bed; they were controlling her agitation and discomfort with medications, and she seemed to be resting peacefully. As far as standing by his decision, he was initially told she would probably only last two weeks without artificial hydration and nutrition, and so he diligently watched over her care. When she went past the anticipated two weeks, he called to tell me he thought the nurses were using too much water to flush her meds, and this was prolonging her demise. He was of course, correct. Continuing artificial hydration even in minimal amounts extends the time it takes for the patient to die, while at the same time, denies the patient any functional ability to enjoy the life they once knew. Once he understood this, his mind was made up, and therefore reported his observations to the head nurse.

Just as he had predicted, he would be by her side and holding her hand when she died, but due to that strong beating heart, it took longer than he had anticipated. Thirty days after her feeding tube was removed, she finally let herself rest, after spending fourteen years in a place for which she was destined. With my granddad's death, our worlds stopped turning for a while, or at least mine did, trying to reconcile that he was gone. *It just can't be.* I thought my granddad would just live on and on. I never pictured life without him, but it was very different with Granny. We had lost her years ago. The burden of watching her slip into a shell day by day fell on my father's shoulders. Oh, the rest of us would visit from time to time, but she wasn't Granny anymore. It became increasingly difficult to look for a trace of something that would bring her back to the way we remembered, the part of her we held onto so tightly.

For all the bad he had observed over the years: the slow decline, the hospitalizations, confusion, forgetting us, forgetting herself, my dad couldn't get past his decision to withdraw artificial tube feedings, no matter how proud I was of him, no matter how unified the whole family was on the matter, no matter how peacefully he saw her go. It reiterated the fact that withholding care (*not implementing* artificial life-sustaining measures) is psychologically much easier on the decision maker than withdrawing care (*discontinuing* artificial life-sustaining measures, e.g., artificial respiratory support and artificial hydration/nutrition), even with the permission and encouragement of the medical professionals. I often wonder, had the staff informed my father of the facility's policy change regarding feeding tubes in end-stage dementia patients, how different the last year of my grandmother's life might have been, how different the rest of my father's life would be. But then, some people take a little longer to say goodbye, and some people have a harder time being told goodbye by someone they'd just as soon not be without.

Though opposites in physique and psychological makeup, different aspects of each other blended them. He wasn't all Barney Fife, and she wasn't all Aunt Bea; there was also a little Pa and Ma Kettle, respectfully. In fact,

Granny was probably more of a Ma Kettle than Aunt Bea, and actually resembled the actress Marjorie Main who played the beloved role of the robust, no-nonsense country woman with so many children she couldn't keep their names straight. Though our granny didn't have fifteen kids, she continually went through all three of her granddaughter's names to get to the one to whom she was talking. Like Ma Kettle, who was the glue in the home, never afraid of a hard day's work, Granny wasn't about fluff or show; she always shouldered her load and kept us laughing at her sometimes brusque way of attacking work and play. If she wanted to eat, she picked it and fixed it. If she wanted fried chicken, she went out and wrung its neck; in fact, one day my dad arrived at her house to find her in the kitchen preparing fifty chickens to "put up" in her deep freeze. He said her arms were bloodied from the chickens' clawing her arms as she swung them around mid-air before snapping their necks—all in a day's work.

And though Granddad was not at all lazy like Pa Kettle; he resembled his humble little frame, and he exhibited the same gentle nature when it came to kids and folks in general. His nickname was Bub—he was fondly called Uncle Bub by many of the distant family, though he was Granddad to four of us who will always remember him as such. He taught us to climb through a barbed-wire fence, to feed a motherless calf from the bottle, to call the cows in for supper, to drive a shift, have fun and laugh. He taught me to skip, holding my hand in his. He taught me the value of honesty, whether by a man's word or how he treated others, and he taught me to sing, though he couldn't hold a tune, because he had a lift in his step, a whistle and an insatiable appetite for living and enjoying others.

Perhaps that is why, at the end of the bike trail where pasture lands come into view after pedaling through dense foliage, I pause and stay for a while. Almost like an obsessive-compulsive drive of will, I cannot continue my ride home until I see the black cows silhouetted against the late-evening sun. They are grazing somewhere out in the pastures delineated by stretches of old barbed-wire fences, and I have to locate them before I leave. When I do, I feel the linoleum under my feet, smell the vanilla wafting out through the kitchen window where Granddad's wheat fields are waving beyond the back fence. It is lowering time on the farm when the cows are heading for the barn, and he is finishing tasks before heading to the house for supper. We are playing as hard as we can in this golden light before being called to wash up. If I stay a little longer, their voices fall soft upon my straining ears.

"Granny, tell us one of your stories!"

"Oh, you've heard plenty of those stories. I don't have any more."

"Granny, please! Tell us the one about Daddy and the ice."

"Oh, I've told that one fifty times. I've got work to do—y'all get out of here."

"Please, Granny, please!"

"Well, okay. One day I was having company over that afternoon, and I needed some ice for my tea. I told Vinson to go down to the store and get me some. He had a little friend named Darlene that was over playing. Since the store was a long way off, and it was hot that day, I told them to take the little red wagon so they could carry the ice back home in it. They sold ice by the pound back then, and I knew it would be too heavy for them to carry, so I told them to be sure and take the wagon. "No, we'll be fine," they said; "We don't want to take the wagon." Well, I got busy in the house and, after while, they came walking up the dirt road with no ice. I went out and said, "Where's my ice?" Vinson said, "They didn't have no ice today." "No ice?" "No, they didn't have any." I whirled around and said, "Darlene, where's my ice?" "We throwed it in the ditch," she said. So I went off down the road with them following me, and, sure enough, there it lay in the ditch under the hot sun. They'd made it about a third of the way home before they decided it was too heavy to carry all the way. I gathered it up and took it home. I dug out what I could and put it in tea glasses, but when I poured the tea, the dirt that had seeped in the bag filtered out and settled in the bottom of the glasses, and it wasn't fit. I had to serve ice tea that afternoon without ice, 'cause they wouldn't take the wagon."

Chapter 4
People Next Door

Although Mrs. Wilson was my first neighbor, it's difficult to say whether she was my favorite. My family lived next door to Mrs. Wilson for seven years until we moved to another town a whole hour's drive to the west, during my first-grade year. After we moved, she didn't reside much longer in the immaculate three-bedroom yellow-bricked house—next to our pink brick—before moving into a new nursing home on the north side of town. I visited her there only once and happened to arrive during the early evening meal. It didn't seem right that she was seated at a table with others in something that resembled a school cafeteria, rather than having her meal served on a metal TV tray while sitting in her favorite comfy chair. She was harder of hearing, seemed more agitated (or as agitated as she used to get with me if I threw a ball in the house), and her hair was bobbed really short, combed straight and held off her forehead with a bobby pin, instead of the styled gray waves I remembered. She wore the same thick silver-rimmed cat-eye glasses but didn't seem to see out of them as well or look at me the same. I don't think I have a picture of Mrs. Wilson anywhere, yet I remember her and the contents of her house so well.

    The floor plan of her house was the same as ours, but it didn't seem the same for various reasons. Her living room was elegant, untouched and quiet. A yellow couch with textured pillows, always in place, and a coffee table with some kind of orange-lacquered floral and ball motif were surrounded with prints and one of those wall clocks with metal arms radiating from its center. I was not allowed to play or even stay in there for long, but I flitted through daily nevertheless. Her kitchen had linoleum floors the same as ours, but the light never came on when you opened the refrigerator, and it was always full of those little clear glass leftover containers with their matching lids. On her wall hung a standard four-piece collection of copper Jell-O molds that, at the time, every house seemed to have (excluding ours, in which Jell-O was seldom made). I spent most of my time in one of the three bedrooms that had been converted to a television sitting room since Mrs. Wilson's stroke. Contrasting comfortable rocker chairs and a black metal TV lamp was all I recognized of hers when I visited her for the last time in her new residence.

Posh instead of elegant described the living rooms of both my new next-door neighbors after moving on Hunt Street, in what felt like a new time zone. Just seventy miles from my first home with a population increased by 10,000, Sherman was graced with finer and bigger homes that sported front doors with decorative multi-colored glass windows, which we would never own. In fact, years later when a next-door friend moved to newer neighborhood with one of *those* doors I felt a pang of jealousy just standing outside ringing her doorbell. Sherman had sidewalks, curbed streets, a giant public swimming pool instead of a public wading pool and showed signs of embracing the late '60s, whereas Paris, Texas, did not. My next-door neighbor was, above all, D-I-V-O-R-C-E-D, as Tammy Wynette would say, with grown teenagers. She was in the process of moving, so she wasn't a neighbor for long, but my relationship with Miss Peggy of Miss Peggy's Dance Academy was just beginning. She would be my ballet teacher until I thought I had outgrown such stuff upon entering my first year of junior high. She had a fluffy white rug, modern furniture and hanging glass lamps that reminded me of Eva Gabor's apartment in the opening credits of *Green Acres*. The neighbor on the other side also sported curvy vinyl chairs and hanging light fixtures while our first "formal" living room sat empty with nothing but dated carpet; we had a lot of catching up to do. But posh could not hold up to the fun that was about to move into Miss Peggy's house as she exited for her new apartment on the other side of town.

The Cabezuts arrived one day in a red station wagon driven by another divorced mom, Martha, with her four teenagers and their four corresponding dogs. Let the party begin! Martha Lou was the oldest and looked the most like her mom, sporting the same red hair, though not as fiery as Martha Senior. Jo Ann was the next in line. She, in time, became my favorite. A little on the chunky side, she sported a flipped hairstyle with bangs and natural blonde highlights that framed her blue eyes; faint freckles sprinkled lightly across the bridge of her nose. Paler in skin tone than Martha, she was easy going and laughed often, except when fighting with her younger brother, John. John looked least like the rest of the Cabezuts and therefore gained the attention of some of the girls with whom he went to school. He had dark eyes, jet-black hair he kept cut short and was tanned all the time. He was of good build and immediately recruited by the coaches of the freshman football team. Kenny. Kenny brought up the rear and favored Jo Ann slightly in body build and sense of humor but was a whole other breed. Kenny also had jet-black hair but wore it like Moe of the *Three Stooges*. I can't remember the color of his eyes, because they were overshadowed by huge, rectangular black-rimmed glasses.

The most startling change that the Cabezuts brought next door was the presence of four dogs to the squared-off backyard that resembled the rest of the lots on Hunt Street sequestered within cyclone fences. I loved the chaos the Cabezuts seemed to bring with them, and their legacy would remain with me, literally, after they moved away. But, the dogs were where it all started. All the Cabezuts had their own dogs, including the mom, but hers was an apricot-colored poodle that stayed inside. I can't remember the names of Jo Ann's or Kenny's—though I think one was a beagle mix—but I fondly remember John's dog named Butch (an old skinny black mutt with a gray mustache) and Martha's—which is strange in the sense that I hung out with Jo Ann and Kenny the most, but Martha's dog would be the reason for our introduction.

Martha's dog was Hector, an apricot-colored poodle mix, whose long hair remained matted all over and continually in his eyes. Unlike the other dogs, who seemed to revel in the noise they created, Hector stood alone against the fence, looking longingly into the starkness and quietness of our yard that did not contain a dog. It was across the fence that I first met Martha.

She had shoulder-length auburn hair and was dressed in a sweater and matching A-line plaid skirt. She was killing time in the backyard, waiting for her mother to return from work to take her to a doctor's appointment. It was the first time I had ever heard of a dermatologist, and the first time I had ever heard of dry ice being applied to the face for treatment of something called acne. She quietly introduced herself and told me Hector was her dog. She was the first one in the family to bring me into their home. I was ecstatic, because she was a teenager on top of being friendly; it harkened back to the days of living across the street from the Aylors. Martha showed me her room and genuinely showed an interest in me but would soon outgrow me, once the school year cranked up. I would become a common fixture in the Cabezut household, popping in on Jo Ann and sometimes watching TV ad nauseam with Kenny and her: one *Perry Mason* rerun after the other on summer mornings. But it was within the walls of the Cabezut house that I first became aware of real changes taking place in the world around me. Martha was the catalyst that caused me to sit up and take note.

The Cabezuts' back bedroom, which belonged to John and Kenny, was the place to hang out for good times and music. They also had their own bathroom, well-remembered because they spray-painted the commode seat gold. Against the wall, sat the chest of drawers they had stolen from Jo Ann. One day, I arrived to the sound of commotion and Jo Ann's tears. She was desperately clinging to a small wooden chest containing four drawers, no bigger than the one in my own bedroom, while John and Kenny were intent on wrenching it from her arms. They overpowered her and took it to their own room, where it stayed from then on, much to my dismay. I kept waiting for Martha Senior to hand down some justice but eventually figured it must have been meant for them from the start. Poor Jo Ann. In John and Kenny's room, the people next door began to grow up within a rapidly changing world, with me looking on.

Martha had a boyfriend and was no longer a redhead. Her acne cleared, she had gone dark brunette and wore her hair in a short bob with bangs, resembling the British trend. At the ripe young age of eight years old, even I understood the connection, since I had seen the movie *To Sir, with Love*. Martha's middle name was Lou, not named after but certainly reminiscent of the red-headed actress and singer, Lulu, who sang the movie's theme song, wore mod clothes, big hoop earrings and white frosted lipstick. Martha and her boyfriend, a blond with dark glasses, would stroll hand in hand down our street, oblivious to my presence, in their matching outfits of black turtlenecks and bell-bottom jeans. And there was something else even more significantly British.

While Martha and her older boyfriend lay on the bed holding hands, the music blared from John's turntable and filled the room. A black 45 with a green Granny Smith apple sliced down the middle turned around and around. The song was "Hey, Jude" by the Beatles, a different Beatles than the ones who played on my old Phonola since I was five years old; this was no "I Want to Hold Your Hand." "Hey, Jude" was not only repetitively called out or "screamed" over and over on the record itself, but because John kept resetting the record needle, those words played over and over. The background noise of my world was different now, just like Martha's, only I was becoming old enough to understand why it was different in a bigger sense.

Vietnam had been a part of my life since as long as I could remember. Pictures of Saigon flashed across the TV screen nightly during the six o'clock news. A continual drone about the Paris Peace Talks played over the car radio between songs. It was as natural as those combat shows my dad watched weekly on television. The guys always started out in the beginning of the show with fresh helmets covered in fishnet. By the end of the show, the netting was torn and the soldiers had blackened faces and necks. Always. It was just something that we lived with, that played over the airwaves, that came into our living rooms and mingled in the conversations around us. It was 1968, and even though I didn't understand everything, the four lads from Liverpool signaled that times were changing; my country and I would never be the same.

One day the Cabezuts left just as abruptly as they had come. They all loaded up in the red station wagon headed for a vacation to California, or so we were told. Not too long before that happened, a man had come to visit for a while. Supposedly he was Mrs. Cabezut's brother-in-law. When they didn't come back from their "vacation," he would give updates on their extended leave and pending return, but, after a time, it became obvious they weren't coming back. Years later, I figured that people will go to all kinds of extremes to get away from somebody, brother-in-law or not. They did leave a few things behind that reminded me often of their short-lived time next door.

Hector had climbed over the fence one too many times and one day just decided to stay. The understanding was mutual on both sides of the fence—Martha had outgrown Hector. I had a new best friend, the first dog I could call my own, and one that would give my dad fits over the years to come. Because Hector could climb a fence (he hung his nails in the cyclone fence until he reached the top, then would drag his back legs over and leap down), my dad eventually had to rig a long, high wire from our back porch to the clothesline. He attached Hector's long leash to it like a zip line. The setup allowed Hector to roam all over the yard, provided he didn't get tangled around a tree. He was kept on the line during the night and while we were away at school and work; I say during the night, until it rained or stormed. Hector was afraid of thunder and lightning and would pound on the back sliding-glass patio door until my dad would get up with a rolled newspaper, but he was undeterred in his panic. (Why my parents wouldn't offer to let him sleep inside during a storm is beyond my understanding.) This behavior prompted my dad to put a door on the doghouse, complete with a latch and slide-in lock. In the middle of the door he cut a diamond-shaped window through which Hector could stick his nose. Sure enough, after a rainy night, I would run to the back patio door to see Hector's nose protruding through the opening, taking in the fresh morning air, signaling to all that it was time to let him out!

Hector stuck around years longer than the Cabezuts and left his own set of imprints on my memory: his attachment to my fluffy pink house shoes, begging from my mother every morning at the kitchen table for bites of her buttered toast (when she didn't respond to his satisfaction, he would tap his foot impatiently for the next handout), his matted brown hair continually in his eyes and, of course, his climbing the fence at will. Just like the Cabezuts, he left one day and never returned, but a year or so later I discovered he had sired an heir on the next street over that looked just like him.

The people next door would come and go, change over time particularly as I grew up, moved off and took up residence in different neighborhoods, different towns and times. It's interesting to note that sometimes the more temporary a dwelling is, by its very nature, tends to lend itself to more intimate contact, wanted or unwanted. Such is the case of a duplex or apartment, due to shared walls—either next door, above or below. Though I would continue to live in rentals for many years throughout my education and career training, some neighborly encounters stand out for one reason or the other. In particular, a stream of people sharing an old house converted into a duplex comes to mind, because it was *my own* first home.

Beginning married life in a duplex was a pretty cool concept on the outside. It was so hippy Carole King style, with my macramé plant hangers, an old footed bathtub, original wood floors and a small kitchen wallpapered in big, bold green and red vegetables. Maybe it was even more cool on the other side of the walls with all the free love going on, people coming and going between the three girls who lived there semi-permanently. But as the voices of people married *to others back home* were overheard from the enclosed back porch, as my own marriage fell into disarray and new neighbors appeared in the spring, it was not so cool. In fact, we were about to face the hottest summer on record, which prompted us to beg for a window air-conditioning unit, just before the heat wave hit that brought all the grasshoppers and finished us off for good.

Our new neighbors were a couple, one of whom I recognized from high school. He graduated three years ahead of me and was renowned for not only becoming the first black head drum major at our high school, but by far the coolest. In the days when drum majors actually led the bands onto the field instead of directing from a podium, this guy not only carried the baton, he strutted the damn thing. One of the best routines the band ever did was to feature his athletic prowess upon entering the football field at the beginning of half-time. In the fall of 1975, the SHS marching band stood tightly packed in the end zone and began simultaneously running in place at the sound of the whistle. From somewhere deep in the mix, this tall statuesque black student in uniform came running through the middle, parting them like Moses. He ran to mid-field, parallel with the turf at an angle a little above 45 degrees with that baton held out in front, leading the band running in formation, before coming to an abrupt halt. I don't remember the song they played next, but I'll never forget that entrance.

Flash forward four or so years, and he's living next door with a red-headed girl. Still enamored with his high school legacy, I went over to say hi. He was on the couch—taking up the full length, of course, due to his height—high as a kite, with his eyes barely slit open. I made some kind of stupid small talk and quickly excused myself, plainly recognizing the reason for all the chaos and noise that happened on the other side of the wall when he returned home from working the late shift. Her blackened eye and quiet demeanor spoke as loudly as the drums he used to pound. The problems that we sometimes face after life in high school began to drive me toward the other side of town.

Moving into another older frame house (without a duplex) was the next best thing my in-laws could offer me, because they had no control over their son's problems and the trouble brewing in our marriage. In fact, my husband spent less than a month there before leaving; it wasn't permanent, but it would only be a matter of time. Prior to moving in, we had painted the kitchen cabinets celery green to match the new indoor-outdoor carpet laid down. My macramé plant holders hung in the side window above a stack of coke cases that held my other potted plants. It was home for a time, away from the thumps in the night occurring through thin shared walls. I slept better, even with the rattle of night and early morning trains on the railroad trestle behind the house. The story of that year is another tale all together, but, the following spring, a new neighbor appeared on the list of next-door acquaintances who surprisingly embedded herself in memory as one of the more remarkable ones.

People or places associated with the very best or worst of times seem to stick with us regardless of the time spent with either. Such was the case in the spring of 1981. Still married, I found myself living alone and pregnant on a street in a neighborhood I had admired while in high school. Driving around in my second- or third-hand car through older neighborhoods with my radio on was a favorite pastime. Whether it was driving by the house of someone I'd had a crush on or merely imagining the lives of those behind doors and lamp-lit windows I didn't know, both narratives kept me driving down streets that were unfamiliar. Such was Elm Street, a sloped drive that eventually ran down to the major highway that intersected the center of town. Many people traveled the part of Elm that connected Washington Street with the downtown area, particularly if they used the bank located on that corner or went that way to pay their gas bill. But few people noticed the tail-end of it, which veered off to the right before crossing the railroad tracks. The street ran between older framed houses that seemed to be on stilts, because they were built on the side of a hill. I accidentally discovered it one day and loved the look of the houses, nestled against the tracks and rushing highway, their backs hidden from the rushing traffic by the lush undergrowth and tall canes that grew in the shadow of the railroad trestle.

I had endured a miserable winter wrought with nausea and vomiting, day and night, due to my surprise pregnancy that announced itself just prior to Thanksgiving. By this time, my husband was living in another town closer to extended family. I had asked a cousin of mine, Diana, if she wanted to move in and share the rent; she was working part-time and going to school. She awakened every morning to the sound of my vomiting in the toilet—before and after brushing my teeth—before I left for work. A short time later, my husband was emergently committed to a VA mental facility, and my cousin stayed on, until he returned six weeks or so later. His home-stay would be short-lived; he returned for further treatment, and I waited out the pregnancy alone, crossing my fingers he would be home in time for the summer delivery, and with sound mind.

Hope began to emerge in the spring of that pregnancy, possibly due to changes that occurred as a natural course of the season. For one, I began to feel better: my nausea had somewhat abated, and the life inside me began to stir and bring just a little anticipatory excitement. Things began to bloom around the house, with and without my aid. I tilled the front flower bed to plant some tomato plants and hung a basket of petunias from the front porch, but, all on its own, a beautiful orange vine began to grow alongside the house. Because my house stood slightly higher on the incline of our street, the windows of my kitchen and side room where my plants hung looked down on the house to the north, an older framed construction painted pinkish-tan with dark brown accents. It was in a somewhat dilapidated state compared to the rest of the houses on our street. The orange vine that grew up from a bush beneath my window gave me something to look forward to, and the house beyond it soon began to take on a life of its own.

Around the corner from the end of our street stood a large colonial house that had been converted into a House of Hope drug rehab and halfway house. It became part of an expansion project for a drug and alcohol rehabilitation program that bought and inhabited some of the other houses on the street. Eventually a permanent structure was built on the corner for offices and meetings. Out of this growing community came my new next-door neighbors toward the end of spring.

• • • •

54 The People of Nineteenth Street

He was tall with a head of rust-colored curls that gave him a touch of youthfulness, despite his often haggard face and worn, dirty jeans and work shirts. She was petite and skinny with long, straight brown hair, olive complexion, blue-green eyes that spoke as gently as her voice. And there were kids—lots of kids who ranged in age from diapers to early elementary years. They were a mixed lot of older sisters who put up with little brother. With the coming of summer came the sound of children out back and the repeated slamming of the front screen door. As their play and make-believe reached a high pitch of whine and argument, their mother tenderly called to them through the back door, reminding them of fair play with patient responses to their pitiful cries for her to side with their cause. As the summer heated up, so did the slamming of the front door, but not on account of the kids.

All too familiar with trying to help people who couldn't or didn't want to help themselves stay straight, healthy, compliant, etc., I felt a sympathetic tension begin to rise within as I watched a sinking ship next door. From the raised voices to late-night comings and goings, I knew it would only be a matter of time before the house next to mine would be vacated and life would resume its usual pattern for the fractured family, unless drastic measures were taken to cut the cord that threatened to strangle them all. The latter choice was eventually made, either intentionally or by natural consequences that follow dependency. Quietness and calm out my window increasingly coincided with his absence. As my pregnancy continued, even the sound of the children's voices eventually silenced. I soon learned they hadn't gone far.

I began to frequent an ice cream shop a few blocks away. The weather was pleasant enough, and I eagerly walked to and from my once-a-day hot fudge sundae. The route necessitated my walking down the street where House of Hope and its adjoining neighbors resided. One day I encountered my former neighbor, walking with her children and a very nice-looking man some years older. We stopped and chatted in front of a small framed gray house with white trim and a matching picket fence. He was a counselor at the center. They had fallen in love and were making a new home for themselves and the kids right there in that little house, a block down from the House of Hope. She wore a blue cotton dress that matched her eyes, and she looked almost as young as her girls who laughed and played as she stood talking, still holding hands with her new man whose smile seemed as gentle as her own. My memory of our sidewalk chat is full of daisies growing by the fence and sunlight. I learned sometime later, after running into her several years past, that she had married and helped care for this man after he was diagnosed with leukemia, up until his untimely death. Even after all she had been through, she still looked youthful, happy, and clean.

After the little white house on Elm Street, I lived in an apartment followed by a rent house, then back to an apartment then to a rent house, until, sixteen years later, I finally moved into a home of my own after a second marriage. It's difficult to say whether apartment complexes or rental houses offered the most interesting interactions with people living next door. A string of faces and families pass through my recalling the years of living in either. And there were good times and bad, challenges with both stemming from proximity, location and often due to lack of socioeconomic privilege. One thing can be said for both, the rental life was never boring, particularly when factoring in the variety of people I lived close to during interrupted increments of time. The same may not hold true for all homeowners, but I found that, as my social and financial situation improved, the interaction with my neighbors proportionately declined. Not that I missed a cop's showing up at my door telling me to turn down my music, or another previous neighbor dropping in unexpectedly, asking me to call her if I ever saw her husband driving through the old apartment complex, but spontaneity soon became a thing of the past, and, just like a relationship missing its fizz, I began to miss the connections made on the spur.

Neighbors in neighborhoods have become like front porches with empty swings and old metal chairs. They look so inviting but stand alone much too often. It seems that the more manicured the lawns, the bigger the home (accessorized with a pool in the back) often means, "Please don't bother to knock," particularly when two large palm plants are placed in front of the door as if to bar the way to the doorbell. I always dreamed of living in a house like the one in which I now reside, but I often drive down streets far away from my own, to seek inspiration and draw waves from people sitting on front porches of homes far less affluent than the rented ones in which I used to live. It is a hunger for an unexpected friend and some more adventure milked out of this life before it grows too late to walk out my own door.

The people next door left something intangible behind, greater than their remembered faces, front doors and backyard fences dripping with honeysuckle. It must have been something they said, did or added—like a required ingredient in a recipe, that helped to expand the way I look at the world, noticing details that make it adventuresome even in the leanest of times. But thank God for the tangibles as well.

On my shelf sits a little book by Thornton W. Burgess, *Mother West Wind "How" Stories,* copyright, 1916. Weathered and read, the spine is taped to hold it together. The children's book of fictional tales relays how certain animals in the Green Forest and Green Meadows came to inherit or obtain characteristics, for example, "How The Eyes of Old Mr. Owl Became Fixed." Inside the back cover, under the scrawled word, Cabezut, is a sticker: "You Must Be 21 To Read This Book."

Oh, where have you gone, Kenny Cabezut?

Chapter 5
Clean Up Woman

I wish I could remember her name. She drove an early 1960s red Ford model station wagon. She was the same age as my mom, or possibly a little younger, and she was black.

At some point during the modest lives of our moms who lived on Nineteenth Street SW, they began utilizing domestic help to clean their small three-bedroom homes. These ladies showed up about once a week, as noted by their cars parked in the front drive, not on the curb because our street was fairly busy and there were no designated parking spaces. Word must have gotten around over afternoon coffee visits or through the telephones that hung on the wall just outside the kitchen regarding the qualifications of each and their available days. Maybe Mom got the idea from our across-the-street neighbor Ruth, who once persuaded Mom to sign up as a volunteer for the local Red Cross. (That blue dress with the patch stitched on the front hung in the closet for years, looking as though it had never been worn.) No one ever before had cleaned my mother's house, except for that summer, when it seemed to be the new rave on the block.

Now, Ruth Aylor had always employed a housekeeper, perhaps even more often than once a week. The woman was practically like family and, if memory serves, the entire Aylor household—Jim, Ruth and their four teenagers—affectionately called her Mamie, or something close to that. She wore a white uniform-style dress and kept everybody in line and or at least out of her way in the kitchen. She let me eat brown sugar out of a bowl if I sat on a kitchen stool next to the counter and didn't make a mess. She was known for her ability to run a Kirby vacuum cleaner as well as her ability to cook and keep a house with teenagers running in and out. On days when Ruth had the bridge game at her house, that Kirby could be heard up and down the street early in the morning.

Our housekeeper never became like family. In fact, her help wasn't required for long (after I'm sure Dad added up the cost and savings), but I always looked forward to the red station wagon pulling up outside. And just to make sure my welcome was appropriate, I had been prepared by my parents for her first day in our home.

The little town in which I resided was definitely a part of the segregated South, but even my parents, who had been raised with black and white stereotypes all their lives, recognized the need for decorum and respect. Though the "N" word was not used in our home, (Mom preferred "nigra"), it was, sad to say, commonly spoken in the local dialect and lore.

For instance, my maternal grandmother had a wild black cat that hung out back in the makeshift garage next to the chicken pen, affectionately (or not) called "Ole N-----." I remember the cat, remember chasing the cat and calling the cat, but don't remember feeling ashamed calling it by its name. I remember when a common childhood rhyme used in selecting an "It" for games switched from "catch a N----- by the toe" to, "catch a *tiger* by the toe"—though the choice remained equivocal for some time.

My parents, being conscious that a black person had never set foot in our house and knowing that my only association with black people was in passing or at a neighbor's house with a maid, felt compelled to remind me *not* to point out that *she* was a black person. So, when the day arrived for her to come sweep, mop and dust, I was waiting at the front window ready to meet and greet. I was probably just as excited over the fact that she drove a station wagon as I was over having a new guest in the house. I was immediately taken with the thirtyish, athletic-looking woman wearing pedal-pushers and a smile. In fact, I was so taken that I commented on how pretty (or different) her red lipstick looked over the color of her skin. This remark drew a sharp look of disapproval from my mother and was discussed over the dinner table that evening. "Well, at least she didn't mess up too bad," my dad remarked.

It wasn't that she was with us for such a memorable length of time (because she actually wasn't) that made such an impression on me, but more of what she did and didn't do. She didn't seem suspect or a victim of the times, which were pretty bleak in the early '60s anywhere in the United States and certainly in East Texas. She wasn't docile or meek; she seemed to fit right in. She went about her work with a smile, held her own and never appeared out of place. I didn't perceive her as domestic help. It was just her job, and I was glad when she showed up. I never thought about the side of town she lived on or whether it was different from mine. I never stopped to think that, for a small designated part of a week, she was the only black person on the block, and her red station wagon let everybody know it. What she did for me, however small, is still a part of cherished childhood that left an important imprint.

Ben Franklin's store was one of the coolest places in town, or so I thought. It stood next to the Piggly Wiggly grocery store designated for our side of town—west of the railroad tracks. It was a beautiful thing when the first load of flip-flops arrived on the shelves, announcing summer had begun, or when the boxes of Halloween costumes covered with cellophane lids (so one could see the plastic mask and flammable attire inside) appeared stacked in the front window and aisles. It was to this very destination she promised to take me when pay day came at the end of the month, and I even got to take a friend.

Just the thought of being able to pick out whatever I wanted was almost eclipsed by the fact that I got to ride in the backseat of her station wagon. I felt special and privileged, not the least bit conspicuous or embarrassed. I guess I owe some part to my mom, because gratefulness was always stressed no matter what color it came in. But I credit my own fascination with station wagons; it's just something I've never been able to explain.

Of all the times I couldn't make up my mind what to choose, it had to be that day! When I think about it, I don't remember ever being driven to Ben Franklin's for my benefit alone, rather it was always an accompaniment arrangement. I was usually along with Mom when she popped into the store for shopping, and I just happened to wander over to the toy aisle where I would begin to scheme a plan to get a much-needed outfit for my Barbie, a new cap gun with holster and caps, or some other regarded treasure of the moment. On this day, I seemed to take an extra-long time to decide what would rank special enough to be considered my *treat*. I finally decided on a horse-head hand puppet and a small, amber-colored glass piggy bank.

I can't recall if she waited on me or just went about the store tending to her own needs, but I don't remember being pressured. At that age, I didn't have an inkling of what it meant in terms of cash and sacrifice, the fact that she used her own hard-earned money or parted so quickly from the meager wage she received from my mom to buy me something. No matter the intent or casualness of the gift, that day of sunshine-filled fun, experienced from the backseat of a station wagon that felt more like a coach, was not lost on me. She probably never knew that her gesture would have such a lasting impact.

I was also too young at the time to realize that neighbors and neighborhoods would change in the near future, pending the movement of the former. Though the *new neighborhood* our family moved to a few years afterward was just as quaint in some ways as the one that encompassed Southwest Nineteenth Street, some subtle differences set it apart. For starters, it had sidewalks that ran up and down both sides of the street in front of the houses. No one burned trash in their backyard trash barrel; the streets had curbs; we were sandwiched between two bricked houses instead of sitting on the corner lot; the ice cream truck ran every summer evening instead of the midday snow cone wagon; and most homes contained one and half bathrooms instead of a single.

Within a few short years of moving there, the face of that neighborhood would change as well. Families of kids I emulated and played with daily moved away, never to be heard from again. A man living a few doors down who made a living driving trucks ended up paralyzed after a tragic accident. His once-busy driveway that held his teen son's cars emptied and only on rare occasion could the strange configuration of him and his motorized chair be seen sitting outside on his walk.

Then one spring morning, our next-door neighbor brought over a newspaper declaring the horrific death of our across-the-street neighbor following a fiery car crash during the night. He was a military physician stationed at the nearby Air Force base, and I played regularly with his two girls, one of whom was in my class. Their beautiful mother, who looked more like a blonde Swedish model than a housewife, suddenly found herself widowed with three children in Texas, far from family in Minneapolis. She wasted no time in selling the house and taking her children back to Minnesota. After tearful goodbyes and hugs from the other mothers, we watched their car follow the moving van down our street, in awe of the distance they would travel to an exotic destination that we could barely pronounce. In time, another moving van would bring the first black family into our neighborhood to occupy the newly painted house hurriedly left behind by a grieving wife.

I wasted no time in getting to know the new neighbors. They were a young, educated black couple with one son less than a year old. They had moved from Dallas because of the man's engineering position with a notable company that operated a large branch in our town. He hailed from a family of educators, unlike my own, and, though they were young and this was his first managerial position, it was evident they came from distinguished roots and weren't long for our neighborhood.

She was pretty and nice and didn't seem to mind when I came over after she returned home from work to play with the baby or just follow her around keenly observing how she took care of the house, what she fixed for dinner, sampling her tastes in style and music. So struck by their artistic tastes and educated status, I saw them as colorless until I came in one day while she was styling her baby's afro. Sections of his hair stood at least four or five inches off his scalp while she systematically tamed them in tightly curled rows. I felt as though I had walked in on a secret: their cute little baby had kinky hair just like any black person on the other side of town—the kind of hair that tended to make certain neighbors' hair stand on end. Yet he *was* black. In spite of living in a blue-collared, all-white neighborhood, they were comfortable with being black.

And so, until it was time for them to move to a better neighborhood, I visited the only black family on the block and got turned onto Betty Wright's 1970s hit, "Clean Up Woman." It seemed like every time I came over that song was playing on their hi-fi stereo, and it got in my head, though I never heard it played on our local AM station. It wasn't like Freda Payne's hit, "Band of Gold," that we played ad nauseam at our slumber parties (without a clue of what it meant). "Clean Up Woman" felt more like an inside "black" hit—one I think I would have missed if I hadn't been a regular nuisance of a neighbor.

Years later, I ran into our black neighbor, Mr. Douglass, at a live theater performance at the local community theater playhouse. Though I hadn't seen him in years, I recognized him immediately. He and his wife were active volunteers in the community theater, and he served on the board of directors. Their little boy had grown up and was playing baseball; they had added a daughter to their family somewhere along the line. I gleaned all this information after a very embarrassing happening.

Some recent bad news, coupled with a gastrointestinal virus, had my stomach in such knots that I thought my digestive tract would never recover. I had continued work while advancing my diet, hoping things would return to normal, soon. Before going to see the community theater's play that featured one of my friend's moms in a starring role, I ate dinner with my parents that night and invited my own mom to come along. I was thoroughly enjoying myself when, toward the end of the first act, waves of nausea and stomach cramps began. I sat in the dark, wringing my hands, willing myself to make it until intermission. As the heat in my head began to rise, associated with that familiar clammy sensation, I quickly left my seat and headed for the back door that led into the lobby. Halfway across the lobby area, I began to "lose it," and I continued to lose it as I ran for the theater's main door, bypassing the restrooms altogether. Just outside the entrance, I bent over and continued to wretch violently into the theater's front flower bed for what seemed a long time.

Relieved at last, I straightened up and walked back inside, where traces of my mishap were still evident on the lobby's carpet. I went to turn myself in to the theater's volunteers who were in the reception area, happily filling lemonade glasses and plates of cookies and muffins for intermission, which was to occur shortly. They quickly grabbed paper towels and pitchers of water, running to the lobby to beat the crowd about to exit from the theater for a bathroom break and refreshments. And there *he* was, down on the floor, cleaning up my mess while conversing with others as if it were no big deal; I hurriedly headed back into the theater to catch the last bit of the first act.

For most people, this event would probably prove too embarrassing to return immediately to the scene of the crime, but not me. I exited with all the other patrons as the lights came up, signally we were halfway through the play. I enjoyed a glass of lemonade while munching on a muffin, mingling through the crowd and chatting with others, including my "ole across-the-street neighbor," who had just finished cleaning up after my accident. It apparently hadn't hindered our talking about old times and catching up on the present—some of us have no shame. I never saw the couple again and believe that they moved from my hometown soon afterward. It was apparent they were doing well, were active in the community, but they were bound for greater horizons after having served their time in small-town life.

    My husband has more than once asked me why my outlook on minorities stands in such contrast to the perspective of many with whom I was raised. I would like to think that days spent with others, as simple as a ride in a station wagon, helped me see the world differently than my own family and acquaintances surrounding me. While sitting in sociology class years later in college, an epiphany over terminology struck me as why I believed the way I did; I was formally introduced to the words, *generalization* and *stereotyping*. My sociology professor in a racial relations class empowered me with the language that validated what I had already known but didn't have the words to express. A long time after my childhood on Nineteenth Street, far away from a clean up woman, I finally had been given the tools to define what had been lived out in front of me.

Chapter 6
Thirty Days in a Nursing Home

In the summer of 1979 I found myself in economic dire straits due to a spendthrift boyfriend and my inability to say when. During a temporary break in our time spent together, I sought a part-time job in addition to my full-time position at a local hospital. I started looking in the classified ads section of the local newspaper for weekend jobs that wouldn't interfere with my weekday obligation. The best option I could find was two twelve-hour shifts on Friday and Saturday nights as an aide in a nursing home.

I was not a stranger to this particular nursing home, rest home, assisted-living facility, extended-care facility or whatever other title comes to mind, for my grandfather had been a patient there for a brief time shortly before his demise. I was also not unfamiliar with nursing homes in general; like my history with funerals, they both seemed to be standard places of gatherings and visitation when I was a child. Whereas funerals and "family visitation nights" at the funeral home varied as to the time, visitation at the rest home typically took place on Sunday afternoons. It was common for me to walk up and down the halls of such a place, check out the cafeteria and lounge area while my parents visited with some of our beloved extended family in their rooms. After dutifully saying hello to my great-grandmother, great uncles or aunts, extended cousins and so forth (regardless of their competency), I filled the rest of my obligated time by looking in on others—from a distance. This could prove to be a little scary, even exhilarating at times.

It's funny to look back on these times as a child and realize that the smell inside the nursing home was not as noticeable or formidable as the sight of the wheelchair-bound and bed-ridden forms. One woman, whom I noticed had been moved to several different "homes" at different times, haunted my sleep one night in such a vivid dream, I have never forgotten it. She apparently had been born severely handicapped from cerebral palsy. A curly-top, she always had a smile on her face and tried to communicate socially, though her static injury would not allow her to be understood. Years after seeing her for the last time, her little petite frame, curled in her wheelchair, awoke me in a sudden sweat of terror.

In my dream, I followed a long line of women sitting in a chain of chairs, deep in travailing prayer over someone in a room where the line of chairs ended. When I got to the doorframe of the room, I recognized her immediately, writhing in the middle of the bed while surrounding women prayed in anguish. Their heads were down, their arms on the back of the preceding chairs, their prayers so intense that their burdened force moved the chairs closer together, closer to the edge of the bed. I was not experienced medically at the time to realize I was probably witnessing a seizure, rather than watching someone possessed by evil while the prayers of the fervent tried to save her.

I recall being more fascinated by her as child than afraid, but, then, I did observe these people from a distance—if I could help it. One Sunday I happened not to be the only kid *visiting*, and this proved great fun. Some relatives from my dad's side of the family came to see my great-grandmother and brought along a cousin of mine whom I had never met and have not seen since. He was a nice boy with Brylcreemed black hair, dressed in proper Sunday attire. I didn't care that he was a couple of years younger; I had someone with whom to roam the halls, and we did. We ran excitedly more than walked, in and out of the exit doors and around the whole place until we got the scare of our young lives.

While walking toward an exit located at the end of a patient corridor and dutifully looking in every room along the way, we were startled by a little elderly black man sitting on a bedside toilet, silently motioning for us to come into his room. The sight of his bony finger, crooked and calling us hither had us sprinting toward the exit door, barely suppressing our screams and giggles. Even so, I recall our going back for another look! The poor man probably needed assistance but instead managed to scare two little inquisitive white kids and consequently make their obligated Sunday visit something worth remembering. He did not, however, cause me any subsequent nightmares.

As I grew older, the sights and smells of a rest home were something I tried to avoid until the time came for close family to take up permanent residence there or until the necessity for money had me applying for a job in one. In fact, the rest home I applied to work in was the one in which I had last seen the little curly haired woman, but I had forgotten about her by the time I pleaded for the job.

    The Chapel of Care nursing home sat just off the town's main business highway. I began my weekend shift at 7:00 p.m. on Friday, after getting off from my fulltime job around 4:00 p.m. This gave me enough time to go layout in the backyard sun and grab something to eat before I reported for duty. I worked the 7:00 p.m. to 7:00 a.m. shift Friday and Saturday nights. Though the work as an aide was not difficult or demanding, it did require some stamina to stay up and alert all night during the silence of the sleeping patient hall.

    I was not inclined at this point toward patient care as a career, but, with both eyes open, I got a good look at nursing care with all its characteristic strong points and flaws. Like most glass-half-empty people, the flaws left more of an impression on me than the nurturing ideal of a nursing staff.

    The LVN I was assigned to work under filled me in on the "politics" of the place on my very first night. We were overseers and responsible for the care of a higher-functioning area located at the back of the facility. Most of our patients were mentally competent and able to get around on their own with minimal assistance—some with the aid of a walker or wheelchair. Other than answering call lights and distributing scheduled or as-needed medications, our main priority was to remain alert and be available for patient assistance. This proved harder than it sounded around 3:00 a.m. on a Saturday, when all was quiet accept for the occasional patient who couldn't sleep and would visit the nurses' station to shoot the breeze about something that happened fifty years ago.

    During my initial hour, a spry little friendly nurse dropped by our station to introduce herself to me and check on how things were going. She seemed likeable and genuinely interested in my employment there. As soon as she left, my co-worker let me know *she* was merely snooping instead of intentionally welcoming me on board. Apparently, this informant had lunch every day with the owner of the nursing home and came prepared to dish on anyone about anything deemed worthy of gossip or involving disloyalty to the establishment. Basically, the LVN meant, *Don't let her catch you with your head down on top of the desk around 4:00 a.m., which is probably about the time she will casually walk back through.* And so began one month of observation and service I will never forget.

It's hard to say if the month I spent working there was a precursor to my future in medicine, but it surely left an impact on me, particularly in the realm of the elderly and isolated. Several incidents validated what I was told later by medical staff regarding chronic-care settings: "Your loved ones will receive better care if you visit them regularly, and you hold the staff accountable for their general welfare." This was sadly evident by the way some nurses responded to their duties.

Only one physically and mentally incompetent patient resided on the floor; he had to be cleaned and changed every morning. We would don our gloves and walk to his room as the other patients were beginning to stir. (During my first shift, I learned that the nurse was re-using the same pair of gloves; I acquired a box of disposable gloves from the hospital path lab where I worked during the day and brought it to the nursing home the next night.) I assisted her by holding the patient on his frail side while she cleaned him. Not an enjoyable task by any stretch, she would complain harshly about his being stiff and not turning for her, as she handled him roughly in the process. Years later while working on the neurology floor of the VA hospital during a medical school clinical rotation, I encountered a similar gentleman who could not communicate due to some previous neurological insult. Standing with the team viewing his CT scan that revealed large dark holes where brain was supposed to be, I thought of my old patient, being turned roughly and spoken to frustratingly, all because of the inability to carry out the basics of his existence due to absence of his gray matter. Perhaps even sadder were the cases of patients' exhibiting fear and uncertainty during the hours before dawn, finding little in the way of comfort in a nursing home ward.

One night I worked with an RN who was filling in for my usual superior due to illness or conflict. She was a no-nonsense redhead who wore her white nursing uniform proudly displaying all her medals up front. I accompanied her to an elderly man's room one night after his patient light signaled. The man was having chest pain, and he looked frightened as well as distressed. His chart indicated nitroglycerin could be administered for these episodes, which he evidently suffered from time to time. The nurse issued him his pill and sternly questioned him about his symptoms, for he was not immediately relieved. She administered more of his prescribed medicine with an air of impatience and anger creeping into her voice as the man meekly answered. He appeared scared and small in the glare of the room's fluorescent light in the middle of the night—a menacing nurse in white standing over him, clearly put-out by having to attend to his distress, much less address his fear. I soon learned that aches and pains, constipation and snippy staff were not the only reasons for patients' uneasy nights; sometimes it had more to do with whom they shared a room.

Toward the end of my first night shift, patients who could get up and dress themselves slowly began to fill the hallways on their way to breakfast. One regal woman with her silver hair in a smart bun and woolen shawl draped elegantly over her shoulder came out of a door close to the nursing station and gave us a nod as she made her way to breakfast with the others. My superior immediately whispered, "Watch out for her—she's mean!" Shortly after her exit, the other small white-haired woman with whom she shared a room came out as well and bid us good morning. The nurse leaned over and told me how the first woman hit this one; she had seen the resulting bruises. I was shocked; the first woman looked like a Helen Hayes–sort, but I was wary of her from that time on. I became fairly acquainted with the other roommate, because she had difficulty sleeping and would make her way to the nurses' station most nights I was there, chatting with us until her Darvocet took effect, and she was ready to go back to her bed. The nurse had a suspicion that she was afraid of disturbing the mean one and wanted to get out of the room to avoid physical or verbal abuse, or other *distresses of the night*.

The nurse then told me how, one night, this same woman had flown out of her room, complaining of a mouse trying to get in bed with her. "I don't think it was a mouse. I think she mistook one of those giant wood roaches for a rodent; they're big enough!" She proceeded to tell me how another patient, without the ability to speak, had buzzed her one night; when she arrived, the patient was pointing in horror to the aforementioned on the wall. "They fly, you know." Sure enough, I began to see where one or two had been killed in the medicine room. She said, "I just leave them there to see how long it will take somebody to notice and remove them. Disgusting!" She seemed to handle the roaches in the same passive-aggressive manner she did the rest of her responsibilities on the floor—anything to avoid contact with the rest of the nursing staff she held in highest suspicion for trying to run her off.

There were some fond remembrances; I looked forward to taking care of some patients. And from working weekends only, I learned how quickly the patients' circumstances could change without warning. One particular patient I was responsible for dressing in the morning was a tiny woman with Parkinson's disease; she reminded me of my maternal grandmother. While I was busy helping her get into her underthings and bra (which swallowed her, though I'm sure it once fit), her roommate was cheerfully dressing, humming on her way out the door, "Good morning, see you later!" My little patient could no longer speak, but she was very alert and communicated with me out of those bright eyes and motioned with her hands where to find things and what she specifically wanted. She was very meticulous, and her outfits matched right down to the shoes she wore. She sat in a wheelchair when not in her bed, but even so she wore sheer stockings with her dresses that hung on her shrinking frame—like a young girl's playing dress-up in her mother's clothes. My grandmother had been dead for some years, so I enjoyed the resemblance that brought back the nostalgia of being with her all over again.

One Saturday morning I entered the room to dress my patient and found her roommate still in bed asleep, with a raspy sound eliciting from her wide-open mouth, her hair in a state of dishevelment. I soon learned she had suffered a stroke during the week, and, just like that, her life was changed for the rest of her days left on earth. Whereas my little degenerating Parkinson's patient could still sit in her wheelchair and eat her meals, this other patient, who so recently had flitted in and out of the door, was no longer able. In her incapacitated state, she was invariably at risk for a respiratory infection that would surely take her at some not-too-distant point. This immediate annulment of quality, the subsequent risk of infection and death all due to the inability to get up out of bed, was reiterated throughout my years in medicine.

After thirty days of weekend night shifts, struggling to stay awake in the wee hours of a nursing home ward, where patients had trouble sleeping and demanded their prune juice at 4:00 a.m. or their crummy sleeping pills for their "nerves," I traded my rubber gloves for a broom and dust rag. Down the same stretch of highway, I found a job cleaning offices at the local Johnson & Johnson plant alongside a law student who was home for the summer. The job was part-time, started immediately after I got off from my daytime job, and generally took about four hours to complete each weeknight. I didn't struggle to stay awake during my shift; in fact, we got our work down to a routine so that, if necessary, we could clean our designated route in record time. One night my working partner wanted to get home in time to see the president's speech on TV, so we finished in an hour and a half, something we were never able to repeat.

I saw everything—from where the railcars brought the raw cotton bales in on the tracks to top executive offices—while making our way from end to end through Johnson & Johnson, Inc., a huge building that still stands but no longer houses the company that built it and inhabited it for more than forty years. The Chapel of Care nursing home has been gone for some time; not even the foundation remains. Both places helped prepare me for life after high school and boyfriends. By the end of that memorable summer, I had earned enough money to pay off my debts. I visited the Chapel of Care one last time, nine years after I resigned from my month-long stint on its back hall.

During my undergraduate studies at Austin College, I had some required projects in a racial relations sociology class. I was to explore the world of living as a minority by engaging in different activities that included interviews and placing myself in situations and places where *I* was a minority. For help, I leaned on a co-worker at the Holiday Inn private club and restaurant where I worked while in college. Willy was a tall, thin busboy/waiter, and he was black. We went to an all-black nightclub for one of my "minority experiences," which was interesting on more than one account. Unbeknownst to me, he had just broken up with a long-time girlfriend. We turned the heads of some of her friends when he strutted into the neighborhood club with a white chick—no mention of a sociology assignment. But before that, he took me for a Sunday afternoon visit with his grandmother, who resided at the Chapel of Care nursing home.

We made our way to the back of the facility where the cognitive patients requiring less-skilled care still resided. So intent on my *interview assignment*,

I forgot to look at the names posted on the door fronts to see if any of my old patients remained. We had a pleasant time talking about her early-life struggles and the death of John F. Kennedy while Willy helped feed his grandmother her lemon pie. Confident I had enough information for my paper; we bid his grandmother goodbye and headed toward the back exit. On our way out into another bright Sunday afternoon, an elderly woman sitting with another patient in the sunroom said hello and asked if we were brother and sister. Willy and I stopped and looked at each other, grinned, and said, "No, ma'am, just good friends."

Chapter 7
Living with Mental Illness

In November 1979, I stood at a Presbyterian altar in a handmade wedding dress that cost around $115 and said "I do" with everything within me. For some, this might not seem such a tall order; even for me it didn't seem so, despite all I already knew. Only six months earlier, I had identified *this* unknown patient as my boyfriend-fiancé, in the middle of an inpatient psych ward miles from where I lived. But I must go further back to defend my resolve.

In the fall of my senior year, I met a boy. It's funny now to think of him as a boy when, at the time, five years my senior, I thought of him as anything but that. Far from statuesque, I found myself bending my knees slightly so as not to appear taller than the frosted long-hair, clad in dark colored bell bottoms the same color as his eyes. He wasn't talking to me. He seemed more interested in showing off his dog, Reefer, to a mutual friend, but I was curious to know more about his story quickly approaching a tragic consequence.

My girlfriend's husband had known him since childhood, and after returning from an Army stint and life in another part of the state, he had hooked back up with old acquaintances—briefly. His history was marked with some dark times that sparked my imagination all the more. His parents had divorced years ago due to the father's addiction to alcohol. His older brother had gone to live with the maternal grandparents after the separation, while his mom continued working three jobs to provide for him and his younger sister. Once a vibrant and happy boy, the split came in his formative years and, after one too many run-ins with a disliked English teacher, he left high school for the Army. In Germany at age seventeen, he encountered a harsh commander, weed and LSD. These eventually led to a mental handicap and an honorable discharge.

Somewhere along the way, he had suffered a "nervous breakdown" (common term used at the time, when people didn't know specifically what they were talking about but wanted it to sound significant) when he was twenty-one and spent some time in a hospital before being discharged on medication. He remained in a depressed state for some time and chose to live with his grandparents during his recovery. Eventually, his life swung in another direction, where fast cars and run-ins with the law handed him a probation sentence. It was at this exact junction where I first laid eyes on him, and it wouldn't be too long before one more step over the line would land him in a state institution for eight months.

But my first encounter happened before the gavel came down, and I, as a young naïve girl, wove a romantic tale out of this tragedy. Sometime during high school, I had read *The Outsiders,* by S. E. Hinton, published in 1967. Written about two rival groups, the Greasers and the Socs, the story focuses on one of the group's main character and his association with family and friends in the gang. I had stood face to face with one of most charismatic characters in the book, Dallas "Dally" Winston—the most notorious of the bunch, the one in trouble, the one who even caught the eye of the rival gang's main girl, who eventually perished with an unloaded gun in his hand.

The book was adapted for a film in 1983, and I'm convinced they cast the wrong guy for Dally. Although Matt Dillon was all the rage at the time, he wasn't wiry, gaunt enough and didn't have long blond hair to boot. I should know: Dally was my favorite character; I had written poetry honoring his memory. Now, here he was—the embodiment of that character standing right in front of me in the back office of our local Kentucky Fried Chicken, waiting for my friend's husband to finish his shift and close the restaurant. In fact, the parallels between the two came a little too close. Before my newfound crush was arrested for breaking his probation, he had temporarily hidden out in a neighboring state carrying a loaded .22-caliber pistol. (He was soon talked into turning himself into the police.)

There wasn't any more contact, only news through my friend of his pending situation. Still, I fantasized like a love-sick girl, lying on my bed listening to Carole King sing "So Far Away," off her 1971 *Tapestry* album, over and over. That was in the fall of my senior year. By Christmas I had forgotten about him, and life moved on toward graduation. That first little encounter would have probably been the last if not for a shake-up in my circle of support. By the end of the school year, I was hanging with a whole new group of people, and the girlfriend, whom I had only casually known through classroom time, became an even closer confidant. I began spending more time in her home—a young couple's first duplex on the other side of town.

What had begun as a summer of free fun and late nights quickly changed the day he came home from prison and made little haste in reconnecting with his old friends; I happened to be there that night. In fact, our little group had been waiting in anticipation. Nothing special happened that first night. For one thing, he had a ridiculously short haircut that was a real turn-off, a parting gift from the Texas Department of Corrections. He spent a lot of time out in the front yard, soaking up the summer night and his new earned freedom. But, soon enough, we were an item, after running into each other just about every night at our mutual friends' home.

It was the typical story of good girl attracted to older, wilder boy, when young girl's heart is lost, and her brain takes flight. We were both making a new start; it was just that my new lifestyle took on a lot more risk. For starters, I was thrown into the world of rebellion and weed—lots of weed. Although I had started imbibing alcohol on occasion, even got drunk for the first time on Tom Collins at a lake party, pot-smoking was something new and foreign. "Homegrown, "Sensimilla," and the infamous "Columbian Red Bud," were all new terms to me and seemed to dominate the conversation of the guys around us. Meanwhile, my girlfriends were usually trying to locate their missing Bic cigarette lighters while downing Cokes and Dr Peppers. Even though we smoked pot occasionally—usually socially, either at parties or with our guys, who particularly seemed turned on by the shot-gun method—it appeared universal to me that guys were much more consumed with the habit than their partners. It was as if their whole reason for social interaction and entertainment was driven by it.

I was unused to a habit of nightly television or the ritual of taking a couple of hits of reefer to enhance any and every experience, whether listening to music, watching the game, hanging out at the lake or starting the day. The effect on sex I understood, but the cost and emphasis on the regular purchase of weed—whether you had the flow or not—was lost on me as well. Reared in a family of modest means, spending the immediate top off a paycheck for a "bag" (even though back in the day $50 bought absolute top stuff), represented a financial if not moral waste. Pay your bills, take care of your car insurance and spend the rest on gasoline and good times—sure, but not off the top. But, this was a new life, and I wanted to be with the boy at all costs.

Eventually, it would all catch up with me. Pot as a favorite pastime and late nights before stumbling out of bed at the sound of the alarm for a full eight hours of work would flip in more than one way. I was able to hold up my part. I didn't smoke much but was surely along for the ride, because I loved the night life. It felt like my natural rhythm. My parents had always recounted my lying in the crib with my eyes as big as silver dollars into the wee morning hours. Riding as a passenger in my own orange VW bug while looking for a place to have sex anywhere and everywhere in the midst of "spot-lighting" for 'coons, fishing, or dropping in unannounced on reefer-sharing friends was something I could live with—until the screw tightened, and the wheel turned faster. In less than a year, his behavior and the insatiable hunger to keep moving always—whether that meant job to job, friend to friend, or through a series of pie-in-the-sky dreams incessantly talked about but never acted upon—took a dangerous turn.

In Kay Redfield Jamison's book, *An Unquiet Mind,* she describes periods of mania as "the gliding through starfields and dancing along the rings of Saturn." I mistook all this energy and agitation as an imbalance of sugar, lack of balanced nutrition, and too much caffeine to counterbalance our up-all-night lifestyle. To complicate matters, he had experimented a time or two with injecting some speed at a friend's house one evening. I perceived it as something he tried for kicks, not something that would fuel the fire and eventually come back to haunt him in the years ahead. All I knew was that the pace was picking up, and, in the face of quitting his job and friends, his continual explanation was "I'm going to show you. I'm going to show you all." It was said over and over until one day, during an argument while I was driving, I pulled over to the curb as he requested and let him out. I watched him walk off into the sun and pulled angrily away. I don't remember where or how long I drove before I parked my car and sat in seething silence. The same sun I had been staring into peeled back the scales from my eyes, and I thought for the first time with crystal clarity before saying it aloud, "He's sick."

If he had been around his family more, if they had witnessed his increasingly bizarre behavior, they might have been able to intervene, or at least point out the obvious to me, though I cannot truthfully say I would have accepted it at the time. The tragedy of it was, by the time I figured it out on my own and turned around to go back and get him, he was gone. He stayed gone more than a week before he was finally found. Estranged from his family at the time, I took it upon myself to look after his apartment, not before leaving him a note each day telling him to call me. I paid off some of his accrued debt to friends and went in search of recent contacts and places he might have gone. I even took some guys with me and headed to Oklahoma to look for him in some pretty rough joints he had frequented in the past. I continued to work and come and go in my own home as if everything were fine, though the worry took its toll on me to the point of my vomiting profusely more than once while worrying over his safety and whereabouts. The charade might have continued longer if not for his mother's calling me one day, trying to reach him about some insurance matter. After learning of his disappearance, she immediately notified law officials and listed him as a "missing person," something I would never have had the guts to do, knowing his aversion to interacting with the police and other authority figures.

Ironically, he relocated himself without our combined investigative efforts. He suddenly "came to" one day in an in-patient psych ward in a city an hour and a half from where he left. He had hitched a ride with a trucker and was dropped off in the Dallas–Fort Worth area. Unable to pay for his coffee while sitting at some Denny's counter, he gave the waitress a five-hundred-dollar ring to cover the bill and walked out. Details of where or how he was picked up were not clear, only that after being asked once again by the staff, "Don't you know anybody?" he suddenly countered, "Yeah, I got a girlfriend."

· · · ·

"A funny thing happened on the way to the psychiatric floor…" While riding in a crowded elevator on my way to claim my boyfriend, the security guard cracked a joke about avoiding taking in riders from the crazy ward. After everyone exited, and he realized that I was the only one left, and that my destination *was* the crazy ward, he sheepishly smiled and apologized for any unintended jabs on his part. I truly was not offended; this journey was totally new to me as well, though it wouldn't be my last brush with security and locked wards.

If the first time I saw him made me go a little weak in the knees, I surely wasn't ready for the sight of him during this encounter. As I stood talking to the same social worker who had finally cracked his identity, I turned to the sound of his voice, "Baby," and quickly reached to hug this little meek man. He had shrunk, literally, in size and spirit. He was heavily medicated, which accounted for the placid appearance of his face and slow movements. He was wearing slippers instead of his worn boots and bell-bottom jeans accented with cowhide. He was released to me after I was given his medication and referral papers for admission to a VA hospital.

The initial admission to an in-patient facility went smoothly enough. So shaken and confused by the previous weeks' experience, he was anxious to receive some help. The overriding conclusion on his and my part was that he had gotten hold of something that sent him over the edge, possibly some pot laced with PCP, because reports of bizarre behavior associated with the drug's infiltration in our part of the state were increasing. A few days later, we boarded a Greyhound bus bound for Waco, Texas.

The Veterans Administration Medical Center that sits on five hundred-plus acres in southern Waco was built in 1932. It consists of a maze of large red brick buildings with clay tile and intricate stone works that some say resemble the Italian Renaissance style. The loop that runs through the ward treatment buildings is named for Waco native and World War II hero Doris Miller. Miller worked in the kitchen and manned a ship's gun to down four enemy aircraft during the raid on Pearl Harbor. The VA facility was opened to serve veterans with nervous or mental disability and has evolved over the decades to include PTSD rehabilitation programs—including residential, nursing home care for psych-geriatric patients, blind rehabilitation and numerous medical and psychiatric outpatient sources. But for those who live in and around Texas, it is most widely known or referred to as a psychiatric inpatient facility—*Wacko in Waco*. This is where he self-admitted on a Saturday morning. Afterward, I took a taxi and, for the first time in my life, checked into a local motel on my own.

Oh, it was a sweet tragic story. I sat waiting for a table in a Mexican food restaurant that evening, feeling raw and blue, wondering if anybody else around me could guess what was going on in my troubled life. Why would such a young girl be dining alone? Could they read the distress on my face and deduce that I had just blown into town, dropped off my love at the psychiatric hospital, and, oh, yes, I would like to talk about it—after all, we *were* in Waco. Though it wasn't exactly *Go Ask Alice,* it had all the elements of a drama associated with drugs, misplaced dreams and bad decisions. Like devoted fans' believing that the outcome of a game relies on their unflagging zeal, I felt the same sense of responsibility toward this hospitalization's success. Thus, I left on a bus Sunday afternoon, confident in the care he would receive, proud of his commitment to walk this road to wellness—keeping my fingers crossed on the way home. I was nineteen.

By the next weekend, I was on my way to pick him up at his father's house in a little town far west of Fort Worth, Texas. He had grown impatient with the process and left the hospital in an agitated state, which was allowed, because he was a self-committed patient. He had hitchhiked his way but not before jumping from a highway overpass, severely spraining and bruising his ankle. He had walked on it, appearing oblivious to the pain emanating from this swollen black appendage that would not fit in his shoe. I was adamant about going and trying to talk him into returning to the hospital. His parents had out-of-town guests they had been expecting for some time and were mortified they couldn't make the trip back to the hospital. I took my poor mom along; it was a Sunday morning when we left home.

We picked him up from his father's, who was very much relieved to see someone coming to take him off his hands, and traveled the two and a half hours back to Waco. He was under the assumption we were returning to pick up his medication; I was under the nervous, hopeful assumption that the hospital staff would convince him to stay, for he was trending fast toward a psychotic state, if not there already. An on-call physician evaluated him on the Sunday evening we arrived on the hospital's campus. The same staff members to whom he had been assigned the previous week were busy with other patients; he could not just simply walk back into his room, as if he would have anyway. When it was obvious he was not going to recommit himself, after listening to the discourse between the doctor and him, my mom was desperate to leave him there and head back home. I, however, could not; I loaded him back in the car and drove three hours before dropping him off at his apartment. Besides, I had missed him and wanted some alone time, until it became apparent that he was not rational and only more hopped up than he had been previously. I did manage to get him to take his prescribed medication before calling his parents to say he was back.

In the psychological thriller film *Secret Window,* starring Johnny Depp as an author with an inner voice bent on carrying out acts of destruction of which he himself would not be capable, a scene harkens back to these days of unrest. Johnny Depp's character steps out from behind a door to confront his separated wife, taking on the persona of his split identity, wearing a tall black hat. The change in his appearance is ominous, because it denotes a completely different persona of the main character. I had seen that hat before on more than one occasion.

His parents quickly drove over to check on him and were confronted by him striding purposefully toward them, wearing a long coat and black hat with a high rounded crown, in the heat of summer. This was his *Billy Jack* persona, not just an attempt to imitate the vigilante *hero* of the 1971 film bearing the same name. Tie on a red bandana, and he was the *Cherokee Kid*, but later, in complete seriousness, he might turn and confess with utmost sincerity that he was indeed, *Lucifer.* Such is the pain borne from psychosis as well as watching a loved one exhibit its manifestations. But his mother had gained knowledge from the process, and, by the next morning, we were all sitting in a waiting room outside a judge's office where papers for an emergency psychiatric commitment were being signed. This also meant that the county would be transporting the patient as well. Even while sitting there watching her hand him paper and pencil, offering various objects to keep him distracted and preoccupied, like a child in a church pew, I was not the least bit deterred from my commitment to see him through to better days. I saw this as a temporary glitch in our relationship, not the revolving door it would become.

It was a long hot summer that started out slow and arduous but eventually got sweeter and better. Because he was readmitted to a "locked" psychiatric ward, we were not allowed to visit for the first two weekends. All I can remember from our first visit was sitting in a locked private visitation room on the patient floor, watching him rummage around the room, picking up any inanimate object, be it from the floor or a small inspection sticker from the wall socket, and examining it very closely. By the second visitation, conversation was possible as well as discernible, and his general affect was much improved. He was transferred out of the locked ward by the next weekend and continued the rest of his commitment on a regular psychiatric ward where he stabilized and improved daily. As his summer improved, so did mine.

It was the first taste of freedom and reconnection I'd had with old friends and the outside world in a long time. I was too young to conceptualize how consuming a co-dependent relationship could be or how much time could be taken away from oneself. I kept my same job but began to get out more and do things more age appropriate. I took on extra work to pay off some debt I had acquired through his manic pursuits and even earned enough to fly myself to Florida to see family and enjoy a week on the beach. I'm sure my family was glad to see this change in me, for I had informed my mother that, due to current circumstances, my engagement was off. (I had accepted a ring the previous Christmas.) Of course, these changes in me were temporary as well. As he made progress, my weekend visits continued regularly, and our relationship flourished with new plans for the future, sure that everything from now on would work out fine.

Memories of leaving the VA in Waco were bittersweet: the people we left behind we knew we would never see again, for we thought it would be our last stay as well. One of the orderlies on his floor rushed out the door to shake his hand and say goodbye as we carried his stuff to the car. I looked around to say goodbye to another patient we had met the very first weekend of voluntary commitment.

While strolling on the open grounds we met a young-looking man in a wheelchair. He had bumper stickers with SAIGON/'68 and other references to Vietnam stuck on his chair and backpack. He asked my name and got a big smile on his face when I told him. "Sherry," he repeated. "I once was engaged to a Sherry, but that was over ten years ago." His face was as wistful as his small frame, resigned to the personalized wheelchair. The years quickly calculated in my head. It was obvious that the war had split them; he had come back different.

We still had some of the summer to enjoy, so we set out to do just that. He found a good job at a ball-bearing manufacturing plant, and we spent the evenings reconnecting with a different bunch of friends—reacquainting with other high school friends of mine, not his. Amid cookouts, water skiing at the lake and hanging at our friends' house, we renewed plans for a wedding with some minor adjustments: a smaller intimate affair with no attendants save for my nephew as ring bearer and his young neighbor as a flower girl. By early November we were married, ignoring or rather thinking we would overcome the depression into which he had sunk. *I* would help him overcome.

Depression: depression is one those words like pregnancy, sex, parenthood—it must be experienced to be understood fully. One can show compassion in trying to understand or imagine how it feels to be in another's place, but empathy comes with being there and knowing. Certain *trigger* words or phrases now resonate within me when a person describes depression, but, during a much younger naïve time in my life, it was just a word that made little sense while living with a person who seemed to function just fine and put on a happy face for others.

Our cute restored duplex with its high ceilings and wood floors became my prison of sorts. The old-fashioned bed up against the window that was shaded by the large hackberry tree, became inescapable, and not in the way expected of a newlywed couple. Because of his early-morning awakenings (one of the constitutional symptoms of major depression), we went to bed earlier and earlier. He thought this would allow him to catch up on the sleep he was missing, and sleep was the intent, nothing else. Hence, the fun-spirited, free-loving relationship that drew us together abruptly stopped. After work and dinner, it was television show after television show, then off to bed before the news. (At least my grandparents stayed up to watch the ten o'clock news!)

My poor work colleagues would tell me things would get better after I complained about lack of sex, while they complained about having to have sex. "Oh, we were like that when we first married, it gets better with experience." They had no idea; it had nothing to do with lack of carnal knowledge and everything to do with the demon of depression that had stolen not only his sex drive but his drive for life itself. Death was just another word, idea, spoken about matter-of-factly: hit by a train, jumped off a building, terrible car accident. "Who cares—death is death," he would say.

We behaved like a normal couple in front of others, but living with mental illness meant making MHMR (Mental Health and Mental Rehabilitation) appointments, and holding onto them, as well as the scripts we were given, like a lifeline. MAOI's (monoamine oxides inhibitors), considered first-generation anti-depressants, were the drug of choice at the time for treating depression, and lithium was the mainstay prescription for bi-polar disorder. Beginning the MAOI (our savior in a little capsule), demanded daily faithfulness and the patience to continue as directed even when little difference in mood might remain for some time. So, during the long winter, I became the cheerleader, encouraging a hang-in-there attitude while dispensing daily medication. Both of us worked to pay bills until retreating at night under the roof of our first home on the corner of a dark alley.

Compliance versus non-compliance, who's winning and why? Medication was taken daily while down in the valley, hoping things would turn around, until maybe we forgot a dose or two, because it didn't seem to be making much difference, or we started feeling a little better. Distractions from reaching our goal of mental stability and normalcy came in the form of new friends—hanging out at new friends' homes and fishing with new friends. And, boy, did it distract. After the winter passed, as the days of spring began to lengthen, so did the days of fishing. What started out as an outlet (returning to something that once gave him pleasure), became an obsession that did not recognize the boundaries of time. It led him further from the home we were trying to make together. After spending months in the dark, lying in a bed without sex and alone within a marriage, I now found myself increasingly alone, physically. The trajectory out of depression was on the upswing, and he was swiftly moving toward mania.

Urging him to take his medication, the need to come back home and the real possibility of returning to a previous state of psychosis were met with the usual declaration, "I'm not crazy, you're the one that's crazy." Kay Redfield Jamison describes in *An Unquiet Mind* her battle with taking medication in the chapter entitled "Missing Saturn": "In my case, I had a horrible sense of loss for who I had been and where I had been. It was difficult to give up the high flights of mind and mood, even though the depressions that inevitably followed nearly cost me my life... And I miss Saturn very much."

Virginia Chase Sutton, in her beautifully written poem, *Lithium and the Absence of Desire* tells it this way: "You have no idea what you are giving away. Winter's amnesia is coming... the land contracts and flips over. The medications' flash freezes you to winter. After time passes, will you remember the fizz of greenery spilling down embankments, how you once drank from the lake's clear aluminum? Back then it was easy to drown in a cup of water, but this is an unexpected kind of going under. How you will shiver, forced to settle for icy ruin, numb winters of regret."

It took me close to twenty years to understand the difficulty over taking medication prescribed for what ails the soul, even though I had lived it via another person and repeatedly witnessed it in clinical practice watching patients enter and exit the revolving door of non-compliance.

Ribbons: I was speaking of the difficulties of managing family and work with a nurse on morning rounds one Saturday when I realized that the convolutions in my mind weren't so easily conveyed in conversation. She was an older black nurse who had worked in the newborn nursery for years. She had raised a large family by herself when times were hard. While trying to work through this fog in my head, wondering aloud how and when life had become so hard, she kept comparing the price of hair ribbons. When her girls were small, she could buy so many hair ribbons for "such and such price," but today things were so different. My brain already hurt from trying to imagine the challenges she had faced as a black female, raising kids alone and going back to get an education; but her only comparison of today's struggles compared to the past, was the price of ribbon? It was the beginning of a downward spiral that would keep me homebound for two months—dependent on those closest to me, prescribed medication and alternating trips to the counselor and psychiatrist's offices.

In the winter of 1998 I found myself in my own Siberia, exiled to the land of major depression, following the joyful birth of my third child some ten months previous. What first felt like a spiritual onslaught, a separation from God and everyone around me, eventually led me to seek help from a licensed therapist and a psychiatrist. Even though the doctor looked me straight in the eye, the way the therapist had, and immediately prescribed the medication both had recommended, it took weeks if not months for me to buy into the diagnosis. By the time I saw the psychiatrist and obtained my script, I was desperate enough to fill it and take the anti-depressant without a fight. Taking the prescribed medication for my "painful anxiety" was another matter.

In biblical terms, "painful anxiety" is referred to as "a broken spirit." Broken by whom? God? Broken for the sake of punishment or abandonment? Was I evil? Was God evil? Was I helping God by taking medication that gave him an unfair advantage over Satan, being that I was clearly in the middle of a war waged between good and evil, the truth, and what seemed to be the truth? While trying to rationalize the intricate workings of the universe, figure and tabulate God's works and mind, it became next to impossible to sit in a room with others, or move through the grocery store without abandoning my cart and running for the door, careful not to drop the thick Bible clutched in my hands. While everything was black and white—the world around me made stark by a reality that made breathing, eating, sleeping, nearly impossible—medication was a foreigner, a fake, a synthetic intruder that did not belong in the spiritual realm in which I was encased. The diagnosis and treatment did not match the desperation I was living; it was too simple of a remedy to address the mind's entanglements and its never-ending maze of questions. Unlike Kay Redfield Jamison's struggle with medication's "cutting into fast-flowing, high-flying times" and Virginia Chase Sutton's depiction of its "shriveling the shoreline to a smudge," my struggle was with its evasion of the truth, veiling the ugliness of God and me. This was all new to me; I couldn't imagine a continuous circle of distorted highs and life-sucking lows.

The inability to communicate with others and have them also feel the soul's darkness at mid-day, or the terror of awakening in the early morning, never one or two minutes off the same hour, only added to the isolation. If I was the only one who was experiencing such pain, then I must be evil and therefore was surely damned; what else could account for such hopelessness? Only when I began to reach out to others, and others began to recount their own experiences of darkness through descriptive narratives, did I dare to believe I was not alone. I was in my room one night, when my oldest son came in carrying the phone, holding the caller at bay until I answered to a familiar voice from years back.

I hadn't spoken to his father for at least fifteen years and had last seen him in passing, walking on the street, twelve years past. The pain I was in brought back memories of a tortuous time. I had longed to apologize for my inability to understand what he had gone through, my lack of empathy for the nightmare he suffered and my impatience with a depression that seemed to flip-flop into irresponsibility. There was an instant vocabulary bond of understanding between us: "Living in depression is a mental hell, isn't it?" I knew he, more than anyone, could express the reality of what it felt like, without need for further elaboration.

I got more than I gave during that phone conversation. It wasn't centered around my apology for lack of understanding the "thorn in the flesh" he had to live with all these years, but rather a sincere attempt on his part to give advice and instill hope. It was like the word of hope I had received from my dad's first cousin and his wife, Bill and Nell, who had called from Florida to buoy me and let me know I could get through. Recalling the dark days of how they had struggled painfully after the suicide of their son (age fifteen—I was the same age at the time of his death), I knew only too well the hard-earned right in identifying with unexplainable pain, "Believe me, this ole boy knows." Unlike Bill and Nell, my ex-husband's struggle was not situational-based; it was the fabric of his being. And so, when he began to instruct me, "Sherry, you gotta keep busy. That's the key. I get so tired of the devil bothering me, I just finally say, 'Shut the hell up—I've got work to do!'" I knew the battle was still raging inside him. It would be only a matter of time before the pendulum would swing too far on the upstroke, dropping him into despair after resetting the midline.

Eventually, the clouds parted. One spring morning while speaking to my mom on the phone, I knew things were different. I tried to explain to her, "The same questions and thoughts are still here, but I'm not 'submarined' by them." The same truth came over me later that day, as I sat with my dad on the edge of a town lake watching my daughter play. The unanswerable questions that had tormented me for two months, that had plunged me into darkness and aloneness, did not have the same impact. I looked around at my immediate surroundings, noting that I did not have a sudden urge to run and hide, though uninvited thoughts still tripped across my brain. The day was slowly taking on a new look and feel, as the world would in time.

I continued taking medication for a year following my long dark night. I started each day with a prayer of thanksgiving for my time spent there. I learned more from being pushed to the brink of insanity than from any other soul-shake-up through which I have lived, but it is a place I never want to return. My journey was a short detour, whereas my first husband continues on an arduous path that was laid out before him in his early twenties. Many other people face similar struggles. I made a choice to experience gripping highs and lonesome despair with another. Then one day, without choosing, I experienced despair. I cannot imagine life if it was defined completely by this up-and-down cycle, though I was once willingly yoked to mental illness.

Chapter 8
Standing on the Corner

For a small-town kid, the changing world scene in the late '60s was a metamorphosis in more ways than Peace, Love and War. Following the New Year in 1967, our family moved seventy miles west to a slightly larger town that boasted things like a community swimming pool, pizza joints, even a four-year liberal arts college. Oh, yes, and public tennis courts that were not associated with the school district. (I do not recall Paris, Texas, even having any school tennis courts at that time.)

On a one-way street heading west through the middle of town, five tennis courts stood in a row demarcated from Houston Street by a tall cyclone fence. To be precise, they were located on the corner of Houston and the frontage road of Sam Rayburn Freeway. They were publicly accessed; they fronted the Health Administration building but were closely located to the Sherman Public High School. Nevertheless, tournaments were held there among adult tennis clubs throughout the region. In fact, while watching one such tournament, I was reacquainted with a childhood friend from my hometown kindergarten class, whose family were participating in the Sherman-sponsored event.

That day eventually inspired me to talk Dad into purchasing a tennis racket, though none in our immediate family had ever lifted a racket. My cousin Linda, six years older, must have been an added incentive for trying something new, because her name was mentioned repeatedly in family circles for her winning talent in tennis. My racket was a Rawlings brand, purchased from our local Gibson's discount store and signed by tennis great John Newcombe. This very fact made me an instant fan of the player, though it seemed that every time I watched him play he was beaten by Ken Rosewall. Still, I proudly honored Newcombe by reverently handling the aquamarine-colored racket when practicing my volleys on the wall of the garage, aiming above the chalked line representing the net.

One day, a school friend named Patricia decided to join me for a *real* practice session on the Houston Street courts. The location of the courts and my friend's name are both significant, for they remain imprinted pertaining to a life-changing event.

On that particular corner, a series of traffic lights regulate the flow of one-way Houston Street and the frontage roads on both sides of the highway's overpass, running north and south, respectively. Drivers are usually stopped by the first light of the northbound frontage road intersection when heading west on Houston Street and, after the light turns green, they proceed under the overpass, through the southbound frontage road intersection without pause, because the lights are sequenced.

On Saturday afternoon, we were basking in the sun among older and experienced players on the court, chasing more loose balls than we were hitting over the net, oblivious to the unceasing flow of cars and trucks over and around us. The superior feeling of spending our Saturday in a more important, mature way than our school peers was only eclipsed by the *real* tennis players around us. So much so, that when my friend and others turned with a "Wow, did you see that?" I was still transfixed by the great serve on the next court and missed what had commanded their attention. I was left behind as the courts emptied of players, including my friend who rushed to the busy intersection, now stilled by a crash that had sent one vehicle rolling on its side.

I arrived late and had to push through the crowd gathered on the corner to get a look at the aftermath that everybody else witnessed in the making. An older model white pick-up truck lay on its driver's side with a bloody foot sticking straight out through the windshield. This would be a strange sight today after the advent of safety glass in vehicles, but, back then, it looked like a page in a horror comic: a foot imprinting a windshield and cutting out its own exodus to the outside world. Emergency workers were quick on the scene (a red ambulance that resembled a station wagon with the back seats removed), and soon the cries of a baby were heard as a car seat was removed from the passenger side with its blanketed passenger intact and apparently untouched. The same would not prove true for the driver.

I became distracted during the time it took to extract the other victim in the accident, while my friend Trisha migrated closer to the wreckage. While looking off in the direction of the northbound-traveled highway, I heard the voice of a man behind me plainly and without passion state, "Don't look if you can't take it." I turned just in time to see the bloody mass of a woman's head that resembled a *very* fresh mound of hamburger meat being transferred to a gurney, her body covered with a starched white sheet that contrasted starkly against the bloody head. It was a blur for me, as I quickly averted my gaze, but not so for my friend, who came running in a panic toward me, screaming, "Did you see her? Did you see her? Oh, my God!" She basically had been hanging out beside the door of the driver's side and witnessed first-hand the woman's retrieval from the pick-up cab. The crowd broke up little by little as the ambulance sped off in the direction of the hospital up the hill, only blocks away.

Although we returned to the court, the event had shaken us so that we had little interest in resuming our game. So much for talking about tennis with our classmates on Monday morning—we now had something much bigger to report. I'll have to admit, I was somewhat jealous of my friend's position, literally. I knew the only way I could have seen what she had was to have been in the location where she stood and have had it forced upon me; given the chance from a distance, I had quickly and willingly turned away to avoid the full view proximity afforded her. In other words, she had bragging rights. I didn't. But I let on to friends and family about witnessing the event, even so.

The woman survived, although badly scarred, and my friend and I eventually parted ways as time directed us toward different junior highs, activities and interests. But I sometimes wonder if that day had the same jarring impact on Patricia as it had on me for reasons beyond witnessing the gore. For years, it played on my psyche and instilled in me a reactive fear to any visual physical injury or disturbance that might suggest the possibility of distorting a human face. Rainy days made me nervous, due to an increased chance for car accidents. The sound of a siren caused an inner dread, assuming it was an ambulance rushing to the scene of mangled victims.

The year following the car accident, a neighborhood friend sustained a gash over her right eyebrow when she failed to manipulate a turn on a dirt track, astride her Honda SL-70. I was standing in her front yard, alongside her sister Shelley and another friend, when their mother pulled in the drive with the injured passenger. Through the window's glass I could see Donna's pale head resting against the back of the seat, with a white piece of gauze over her eye that resembled a Civil War bandage. I freaked at the site of her ghostly white face and dampened hair. I tried desperately to pull the other friend from the ghastly sight and leave with me, but she said, "Hold on a minute!" I turned and ran home in a panic, only to be called on the phone by Shelley, telling me to come over and see all five or six stitches her sister had obtained from the local emergency room. By the next day, a slim Band-Aid covered the entire area of the injury.

The incident at the tennis courts continued to haunt me for years, even though I was drawn to the medical field as a future destination. The panic of not being able to function in the presence of human trauma caused me to pursue a *safer place* within opportunities offered by the health occupations work program for high school students. My first real job at sixteen had me gathering tissue specimens from the hospital's surgery suite and transferring them to the pathology lab where they were dissected, processed and eventually placed on microscope slides for definitive diagnosis. I was literally immersed up to my elbows in tissue and fluid specimens from the body, while dumping and cleaning the receptacles they were kept in for a required time, but only the fumes of the formaldehyde solution they were stored in bothered me, not the sight. The fact that the specimens came *unattached* to their owners was another consolation; even the first above-the-knee amputation I collected from the surgery suite in a large cardboard box did not bother me. But body parts and their diagnoses separated from the patients and their potential outcomes only held me for so long; one day it became clear that I wanted a more comprehensive place in medicine.

Specimens from surgery were always connected with the patient's name and date of birth. Upon arrival in the pathology lab, they were signed in and given an identification number that would follow them throughout the tissue-processing phase, diagnosis, transcription and final report on the patient's file. Unless something was unusual about the name, age or we recognized someone's identity, the patient was separated from the rest of the process, until the day I heard the hospital speaker page a patient's name. We had processed a series of biopsies that belonged to a young girl; her diagnosis came back as Hodgkin's Lymphoma (cancer of the lymphatic system). Her name had stuck with me because the diagnostic tragedy struck a familiar chord in me.

My best friend had been actively fighting the same disease, off and on, for the past eleven years. She had been a vivacious, twenty-two-year-old when a huge lymph node in her neck turned out to be something serious. The subsequent chemotherapy had been grueling and had changed the course of her life. Such was the case of this girl, only sixteen at the time of her diagnosis.

We were busy compiling the slides and dictated reports to accompany the patient to a referral hospital in Dallas for further treatment when her name was called over the loudspeaker. I caught the widened stare of my lab partner, and we rushed down the hall to see if we could get a peek at the girl whose diagnosis had gripped us. She had just left the building with her parents, and, though we did not get to put the name with her face, the incident served as a turning point. I became increasingly frustrated with not being able to connect to the patients; I wanted to play a more hands-on role. I wanted to see the bigger picture up close.

Night school at the local junior college took on much more importance. I may have been sitting in classrooms with cinder block walls, but I told myself I was learning the same subjects as other students in universities across the state, and if I could just get past math requisites, I could further my career in medicine. After hurdling trigonometry, I was in a pre-calculus class one night when a fellow student told me she was transferring to our local liberal arts university the following semester. It was the first time I realized I could transfer without completing my associate's degree.

Attending night classes after putting in a full day's work, summer classes, meeting pre-med requisites, and more summer classes were some of the most challenging days I would ever face, but each step moved me a little closer to a dream I thought had left me behind: a professional career and title. As the light at the end of the tunnel began to penetrate the day-to-day drudgery of studies, I found myself encountering the same doubt triggered by a gruesome car wreck seventeen years previous.

I had been recommended by a few of the biology faculty members to attend a medical school preview at the University of Texas Medical Branch in Galveston. Though this invitation by the medical school was a chance to promote its program and entice students in pre-med programs across the state to consider the school as their choice of placement, I was humbled and ecstatic just for the opportunity. My efforts seemed about ready to pay off. After completing my two-day stay on campus, I went to visit a friend who was now living in the Houston area. I was sitting at her breakfast table, recounting all the exciting details, when I wondered aloud if this were all for naught. "What if I can't handle it? What if I freak out over what I might encounter?"

My friend Jill had worked in the hospital's medical lab during the time I had worked in the hospital's pathology lab. She had gone on to work in two different doctors' offices and in an emergency clinic before pursuing a nursing degree. She said, "Didn't you hear about what happened to me when I applied for the lab tech job? I accompanied somebody up on the floor for morning lab draws and I passed out and hit the floor during the first needle stick. I came back and sat in Chuck's office (the lab director at the time), and said, 'Well, I guess I can't do the job.' And he looked at me and said, 'Yes, you can!' Sherry, there have been times that people have thrown up or bled on me, and I haven't even noticed. You can do this."

Medical school did become a reality, followed by pediatric residency, private as well as academic practice; but, like most dreams, the illusion of who I wanted to become didn't always match up to my actual role. Although I experienced "I have arrived" moments, I learned some of the most important lessons by being at the right place at the right time: "standing on the corner."

A common saying during medical training years, particularly targeting interns during their initial year of residency is "See one, do one, teach one." This applies to more than technical procedures being taught and practiced on patients; it also refers to the hierarchy of supervision in the medical field. Hands-on training is usually demonstrated and taught by the level of expertise a step or two above the trainee. Of course, while some technical/surgical procedures and patient rounds are supervised by the attending physicians, a large part of clinical experience comes by practicing a corresponding level of responsibility. Clinicians in training are often influenced most by the residents or fellows they train immediately under—for better or worse. By the time residents or fellows of a specialty program near the completion of their study, they become the go-to-person for the medical team. Yet, as many teachable moments—some of even greater consequence—are learned from ancillary members of the medical field and, most importantly, from the patients themselves.

• • • •

The medical team takes on a whole new meaning when the façade of competency in the name of competition is dropped, and everyone works together for the common good of the patient. This can happen when the people in charge allow themselves to seek or accept help from others; putting temporarily to rest the assumption or belief that our greatest strides in medicine occur when *we* do something that displays our medical knowledge and skillful expertise. Pivotal moments occur when least expected, and we feel out of depth—not how we envisioned ourselves in crucial circumstances.

I wish I had been "standing on the corner" during one of my rotations in the neonatal intensive care nursery (NICU). What I once considered an enticing field became a nightmare when I began spending physical time in the NICU during required pediatric rotations and night call. The ongoing stress of managing premature infants on respiratory ventilators, often weighing less than a pound, was only matched by the emergent call to resuscitate one in the delivery room.

A significant part of training in the unit is accessing the child's airway. There is a profound respect for this part of the anatomy in these patients. Tensions during pediatric codes run sky-high. That's not to say adult codes are less traumatic, but the skill it takes to locate and maintain the patency of these small orifices demand focus and repeat practice runs, which is what the pediatric resident during a NICU rotation will surely receive.

What started as a typical call-night in the NICU soon turned cause for anxiety when the attending, as she was leaving for the night, told our on-call team that a woman with unsure dates around twenty-three weeks was laboring downstairs in the OB unit. As the upper-level resident, I was to gather a medical history from the mom to better assess the gestational date and speak candidly with her about resuscitation—that it would depend on the viability of the infant. In other words, if physical signs indicated that the infant was too premature for survival, even within the NICU setting, it would be futile to attempt resuscitation upon delivery. My attending instructed the team to continue to check with the OB floor regarding the labor, to give her enough heads-up to be there to assist me, if I wanted her there. *NO problem*, I thought, *of course I wanted her there.*

An intern, third-year medical student and I were going about our nightly duties within the unit when we were paged to one of the delivery rooms for delivery of a twenty-six-week-old infant. Though it doesn't sound like much of a difference between a twenty-four "weeker" and a twenty-six "weeker" preemie, there is a *huge* difference in terms of gestational development. So, unalarmed, we went to station ourselves next to the awaiting heated incubator in the delivery room, ready to assess, intubate and oxygenate the infant before transporting to the NICU. We were calmly awaiting the delivery when an overhead page called the pediatric team to Delivery Room 4 for a twenty-four-week-old preemie. I turned to the intern, handed her the laryngoscope and endotracheal tube and said, "Good luck! You guys are on your own," as I rushed out the door and down the hall.

I entered the delivery room to find the neonatal team, consisting of three unit nurses and a neonatal respiratory tech, ready and waiting; standing next to the on-call, upper-level OB resident was *her* attending. I was livid. Apparently, they had time to communicate to their staff the pending birth but had not notified me. So, I stood alone and unsupported, especially since our team had been split between two simultaneous deliveries. There was no need to assess the gestational age, for the fetus came out fighting. This twenty-four-week-old preemie may have had fused eyelids, but it was pink and waving its fists.

I positioned the infant on the warmer, like I was supposed to, and inserted the laryngoscope to bring the tiny tracheal opening into view so I could insert the endotracheal tube into the airway. After securing the airway, the infant could be oxygenated by hand with an Ambu bag until transferred upstairs and placed on a ventilator in the NICU, except it didn't go that smoothly. The size of the endotracheal tube was appropriate, but, in such a tiny fetus, threading the tube through the trachea is a challenge. After each unsuccessful attempt at trying to insert the tube, the infant continued to be oxygenated with the bag-valve mask, until a fresh endotracheal tube was handed to me by the respiratory tech standing alongside. After two or three attempts, the nurses began to shift their weight within the silence of the delivery room. The tension was palpable. I began to pray in earnest, *"God, beam me up, and get me out of here!"*

Then, a tall, red-headed neonatal nurse moved from her place at the foot of the warmer and stood directly next to me. She didn't say a thing; she didn't appear anxious; she just stood like a pillar of strength next to me. I could feel it. The respiratory tech handed me a smaller tube, which I promptly inserted into the trachea. "We got an airway," she said, as she syringed surfactant down the endotracheal tube. (Exogenous surfactant is a mixture of protein and lipids that is given as a prophylactic treatment to reduce the severity of respiratory distress, routinely given in premature infants less than thirty weeks' gestation.) While oxygenating the infant through the tube with a valve/bag, we quickly rolled the infant toward the special NICU transport elevator, briefly pausing by the side of the mother, so she could see her baby.

Both babies resuscitated in the delivery rooms that night were placed on ventilators and initiated into the routine of the unit that would become their home for the many months to follow. In fact, I was on another rotation when the preemie I intubated was finally released to go home with her mother. She graduated from the NICU with a host of medical and physical challenges many preemies at such a young gestational age upon delivery encounter. There was not a sense of pride on my part, even though the mom had a big smile of relief on her face as she carried the baby out of the unit. I had worked long enough in all areas of my field, to recognize the adversity this young patient and her family would encounter throughout her lifetime due to her physical limitations. Rather than remembering the delivery as a moment I could revel in as saving someone with my skill; I remembered the nurse who had stood by me.

Some years later after I had entered a private practice, I ran into her at another hospital during morning rounds in the nursery. We chatted awhile about her new position and the nursery that was relatively new. Before leaving, I reminded her of our brief encounter during my training, and how much it had meant. She didn't remember that night, but I thanked her for being there for me. It was a lesson I took away; we can experience incredible events outside of our control when we will ourselves to be still and be a witness.

Chapter 9
The Eighth Floor

The first time I saw a child in the hospital was the day after Darren Fendley had his tonsils removed. In the 1960s, tonsillectomies performed on children were as routine on the surgery schedule as cataract removals are today. And so, I accompanied my mother up the front steps of McCuistion hospital, located next to the Coca-Cola Bottling Co. of Paris, Texas, with present in hand to visit my friend. He was quieter than even his usual quiet self but seemed happy enough sitting up in bed with a bowl full of Jell-O in front of him. I left the hospital that day somewhat miffed at the idea of Darren and other kids getting presents and all the ice cream they could eat over the next week just because their tonsils were taken out; I would never be so lucky. My memory of walking through that hospital's large screened front door contrasts starkly with my first medical school visit to the oncology floor of Santa Rosa Children's Hospital in San Antonio, Texas. I stepped into the elevator with the other students on a hospice elective rotation, and Dr. Primomo pushed the button for the eighth floor.

Dr. Marion Primomo (1920–2014) is considered by many in medical circles to be the Mother of Hospice Care in Texas. A German immigrant who came to the United States with her parents in 1926, she later battered down the doors of discriminatory practice against women in medicine and, in January 1947, became one of five women to earn an MD from Loyola School of Medicine in Chicago. After years of family practice, together with the sisters of St. Benedict's hospital, she established the first Hospice of Texas in 1978. She went on to serve as medical director of Hospice in San Antonio, Santa Rosa Hospice, Family Hospice, and Hospice Homecare. As a clinical professor in the department of family and community medicine at the University of Texas Health Science Center at San Antonio, she became the first teacher of palliative medicine in 2000. When I first met her, I had no idea of her stature as a pioneer in medicine. Physically, she stood barely five feet tall in heels, but she had already made such an impression during our elective that I was excited about closing out a Friday of classes on a children's oncology ward. My best friend's death from cancer the same year I began medical school had not only sparked my determination to pursue a career in medicine, it had instilled an appreciation and awe for the practice of oncology and end-of-life care.

Enter Santa Rosa Children's eighth floor off the staff elevator, and immediately the faces of childhood leukemia and medulloblastomas greet you. The eleven-by-fourteen-inch portraits of children, professionally framed and spaced eight inches from one another on the wall, serve as an instant, poignant reminder of why this floor unit exists. Ironically, the local photographer of these children, Paul Overstreet, would some years later, photograph my wedding. His ability to capture their stories on glossy paper never left me.

Our brief tour commenced down the carpeted hall, past the check-in window for the out-patient hematology/oncology clinic to the office door of Dr. Clementina Geiser. Though the petite Italian-born oncologist was not the professor who influenced my interest in pediatric oncology, she provided my introduction. On this cloudy, late Friday afternoon, Dr. Geiser was our only source of reference into the foreign world we had just entered; most of the clinic patients had left for the day. We talked of bone biopsies and such—the most common forms of childhood cancers and their statistical prognoses. After our question-and-answer session, we boarded the same elevator down to the front lobby of the hospital, straining for one last look at the young faces of leukemia before the doors closed. We did not realize that the in-patient pediatric oncology ward and bone marrow transplant unit were just around the corner and opposite to the hall where we had been. I had just been given a peek into what would someday become my medical home.

The transition from the first two years of medical school to the clinical training years of third and fourth year were just across the third-story crosswalk for students at the University of Texas Health Science Center at San Antonio (UTHSCSA). Looking longingly at the university/county hospital while in the courtyard of the medical school during lunch or studying for a test, I constantly reminded myself why I was there. It drew a yearning from within, as well as a desperate plea to be allowed to cross over someday, based squarely on the results of six cycles of exams administered during those initial two years. The challenges of the third-year rotations, our introduction to overnight call and turf wars between the different programs within the halls of the teaching hospital were meant to guide us into our selective medical specialties. The fourth year was designed to help us hone in on a surgical or medicine-based interest and apply for those residency programs, while enjoying electives and some residual classroom time (e.g., statistics, ethics). Because of a fourth-year elective rotation, my trajectory toward treating adult oncology patients forever changed; I would not be applying for either an internal medicine residency or a spot with an otolaryngology surgical program (due to my fascination with head and neck cancers). As I watched a trail of IV poles—being pulled by the children attached to their port-a-caths—moving eagerly down the hall of Santa Rosa Children's eighth floor to the game room after morning rounds, I knew then where I wanted to spend my next six years.

The fourth-year elective through pediatric oncology introduced me to the rigors of morning rounds on the floor and inside the bone marrow transplant unit, which seemed to drag on for hours. Just before my intern would hit the large button on the wall allowing entrance into the closed unit, she would announce, "Through the gates of hell!" On some days, her descriptive analysis wasn't far off. Kids who were taken to the brink of death after a harsh chemotherapy and radiation protocol prior to receiving their autologous or allogenic (stem cells from a donor) transplant of white blood stem cells were vigorously supported medically until the transplanted cells engrafted, or "took hold." If grafts were successful, the cells multiplied, resupplying the patients with their innate ability to fight infection. During that waiting period, both sides of the patient's bed was adorned with matching IV poles hanging fluids, antibiotics and blood products that resembled an array of hanging Japanese lanterns.

Day by day, hour by hour, minute by minute, the staff monitored the patient's status. Slowly, doctors added a regimented list of antibiotics and anti-fungals to the standing medical orders on the chart as the rising temperature dictated. Along with treating potential bacterial, viral and fungal infections came other anticipated and "not-so anticipated" complications associated with a bone marrow transplant. The most immediate and uncomfortable complication was mucositis: a raw sore beginning in the mouth of the patient and extending throughout the mucosa of the gastrointestinal tract subsisting of denuded (raw) abraded tissue. Unable to take anything by mouth, the patient was supported by TPN (total parental nutrition) through a central venous catheter. If the patient did not deteriorate further or suffer from other serious complications such as liver disease or fulminate rejection of the graft, the management of the patient remained somewhat reasonable, and what was going in could be balanced by what was going out (i.e., "ins and outs").

As complications arose, appliances were added, such as new venous lines—introducing the pic-line (percutaneous intravenous catheter) to transport other blood products or supportive electrolyte volume. A patient's rapidly changing nature made regulating ins and outs increasingly difficult. Greater ins led to the dreaded complication of fluid overload, which could lead to pulmonary distress and other organ damage, due to the kidneys' inability to keep up with the large amount of fluids given in the form of IV medications, nutrition and blood products—the very things doctors were giving the patient to support them. As a fourth-year medical student, I watched as the attending physician would come down on the residents and intern for this imbalance, then watched the interns sit down with the pedi-oncology doctor of pharmacy (Pharm.D.) on the floor, scratching their heads to make allowances for the next day—without the help of a "crystal ball," as our Pharm.D. suavely put it.

After the "fires" were put out temporarily in the bone marrow transplant unit, the team exited the button-controlled double doors, led by the attending physician, trailed by the medical students to round on the patients residing on the pedi-oncology floor. An array of hematological and oncology-related challenges greeted us there as well. They took up every bit as much time as that spent in the unit; they were just spread out over an entire floor. Typically, most patients were in for a round of chemotherapy, per protocols treating leukemia or other solid tumors such as medulloblastoma or osteosarcoma. Hematology patients on the ward comprised sickle cell anemia patients in for pain management due to a sickle cell crisis and hemophiliacs in for complications—notoriously AIDS and its never-ending accompanying infections. The AIDS patients were sprinkled throughout the morning rotations during my fourth-year elective; the following year during my internship, I saw none. They were all gone.

During our fourth-year elective, we listened intently to our attending, followed the orders of the resident, but primarily hung close to our respective interns whom we assisted in retrieving medical histories, lab information, daily ins and outs and vital signs on their slate of patients. In some ways, the medical student is afforded a chance to become more intimately involved with individual patient care, because they are only given a few patients to follow and therefore have more time than, say, the resident who is responsible for overseeing the entire floor. That responsibility shifts in challenge as the patient census goes up or down. As a medical student interested in children's cancer journeys, I was intrigued by certain patients whose faces and stories never left me. One such *short* cancer journey I remember well didn't even involve me: my fellow fourth-year medical school student's patient, Julio.

Julio was admitted to the eighth floor one sunny afternoon just shy of his eighteenth birthday. He was accompanied by his older brother, who served as a translator for his parents, a mentor and an advocate for his younger brother. Julio had been referred after tests confirmed a diagnosis of Hodgkin's lymphoma. He was IV-accessed and primed for his initial chemotherapy regimen to begin that afternoon. Julio's physical exam presented a great teaching case for medical students. He had classic signs of lymphoma, exaggerated by his large tumor load. The lymph nodes in his neck were readily found due to their enlarged presence, and his liver and spleen were easily palpated, which they typically are not—especially for medical students naïve to lymphoma and leukemia patients.

Julio became an immediate favorite with the floor staff and oncology team. He was articulate, friendly and had a passion for art. Like most of the patients at Santa Rosa Children's Hospital, he came from an underprivileged family, but, unlike many referrals, he was a local kid who attended a San Antonio high school. He was openly adored by his brother, who found it difficult to say goodbye to Julio at the end of visiting hours. The call team took over at the end of the day to supervise the oncology team's roster of patients during the night shift. All did not go well.

I arrived at the staff desk the next morning, greeted by the whitened face of my medical student colleague, Ann. "Julio died last night," she whispered. She was visibly shaken. Apparently, Julio's tumor load had been so massive that the initiation of chemotherapy had resulted in an acute tumor lysis syndrome, which caused a dangerously high level of potassium to be released into his blood stream. This metabolic complication led to a heart arrhythmia that ultimately resulted in his death. The on-call team emergently rushed him to the pediatric ICU, where attempts to initiate kidney dialysis to clear the potassium load came too late. Julio was gone. The floor team was shocked; the on-call team was upset by the overnight tragedy, and Julio's brother reportedly wept. Even though he was not my patient, even though I had only visited his bedside once during general afternoon rounds, I felt the loss as well. We were a team.

It was a tough month. If one "sickler" was admitted in a pain crisis, then three or four seemed to follow within the week. If a patient had a chemotherapy complication, it seemed to drag on, such as the case of one young lady, whose body reacted in a fit of pancreatitis. Every morning we appeared at her door with the results of her elevated amylase levels that indicated her pancreas was still inflamed, assuring her the continued presence of an NPO (nothing by mouth) sign upon the door. She remained buried under her covers the entire month, either due to depression, despair, or just plain get-out-of-my-room anger. Complications in the bone marrow transplant unit multiplied upon each other, further challenging the team who held its collective head in frustration while the attending physician seemed to take it all in stride, demanding balanced ins and outs. We enjoyed bright moments as well: the camaraderie, the excitement of participating in clinical practice, and the patients. I would continue to cross paths with some during my pediatric residency while rotating through the pedi-oncology unit; others would complete their treatment protocols and follow-up in the clinic; some would die at home; others would come back to die in their medical home on Santa Rosa's eighth floor. Several I would never forget.

Rose Ann was a spunky, gangly eleven- or twelve-year-old girl whose sense of humor was beyond her years. It seemed to allow her to traverse whatever she was going through. Her leukemia was the AML variety (Acute Myeloma Leukemia), which tends to be more aggressive than ALL (Acute Lymphocytic Leukemia), which is more commonly seen in children. Her previous bouts with chemotherapy had left her heart damaged due to one of the medications in the protocol; therefore, the offending agent's dose was diminished during her treatment regimen. Trade-offs are necessary sometimes: an attenuated, less-effective dose administered for a virulent life-threatening cancer, because the treatment could kill her as well. We could never underestimate this kid. One of the attendings once confessed that he continually looked around while Rose Ann was on the floor, half expecting her to kick his leg out from underneath him while he stood signing charts. My experience with her was refreshingly precious, not to mention downright inspirational.

Unlike the first time I had seen her from a distance—bearing her midriff in a little pink cotton top, chasing her brother around the staff desk—this time, she was being admitted for an infection, and I was the medical student appointed to follow her hospital course. She was a little weaker, her eyes set a little deeper and darkened, but she was still the same mischievous kid. She loved Paula Abdul and spent the day speaking pre-teen lingo with her best friend about boys, music and makeup, though she didn't wear any. Her girlfriend wore tight short shorts, teased her hair, wore lots of makeup and interacted with Rose Ann as if they were sitting in her bedroom back home. One afternoon they wanted to perform a dance routine for my critique, set to the tune of Paula Abdul's hit, "Rush."

I sat on top of the heating/cooling vent against the window and watched their choreographed moves; Rose Ann with her port-a-cath accessed and draped hospital gown dancing in sync with her friend. They performed this alternating move throughout the song. One would crouch and hug her knees while the other continued to dance. Rose Ann spent more time in the bent position than her friend. The friend breathlessly told me while still dancing to the song, "We've choreographed some rest spots in the song, so Rose Ann can catch her breath and no one will really know," as she alternatively went into the crouched position. I watched in amazement at this no-big-deal, don't-feel-sorry-for-me show these two girls put on as they danced to the beat of Paula Abdul on an improvised dance floor housed on the eighth floor. I was so moved that I showed up in her room the next day with a rented video she might like to watch: the *Paula Abdul—Straight Up* documentary (1989).

That was the last time I saw Rose Ann. During that course, she beat her infection and was released from the hospital. She continued her attenuated AML chemo treatments for a little longer. The following year, during my pediatrics internship, I learned that she had died peacefully at home in her father's arms. Oh, how we would miss her mischievous charades on the floor, her impish grin and that free spirit that kept her skinny browned body swaying to the beat, no matter what befell her.

Such was the way of life on the pediatric hematology/oncology ward. They came and went. They showed up for their routine chemotherapy, had their ports accessed, endured the protocol with or without side effects, and went back home. They showed up with their infections, due to their immune-compromised state of being, had their ports accessed for IV antibiotics, and either did well or were transferred to the pediatric intensive care unit. Sometimes they showed up for out-patient clinic appointments down on the other end of the hall. They showed up for staging and reassessing bone marrow biopsies, and spinal taps according to standardized protocols. They showed up for pain management in sickle cell crisis, for management of persistent vomiting and dehydration post-chemo, respiratory distress and infections in the hemophiliac/AIDS group. Sometimes they came back to die, because it was home. They were known; they were valued and treated with respect; and the entire staff, from attending physician to nurse to pharmacist to child-care specialist, was committed to their care. And the families knew it.

When a child was dying on the floor, an underlying nervous tension, almost anticipatory effect lingered, despite efforts by the staff to remain confidential and professional. The nurses asked parents to keep the patients' rooms closed as much as possible, and a nurse was placed in the dying patient's room. Everyone went about their work, and no rushed movements or hurrying was noted. No one was in a panic. In fact, sometimes the parents on the floor realized what was going on more than the residents or medical students, who were busy with charts and orders. An understanding, a common bond of dread existed between the families. After all, they had passed each other in the hall, sat next to one another in the clinic waiting area. They knew.

The experience was different for each kid, for each family even though the underlying diagnosis was primarily oncologic. The dynamic of the family, the age or character of the patient defined each death as special and as unique as the children themselves. I wasn't there for most of them, but the ones I witnessed, I found at some point my attention shifted from the patient to those intimately close to the patient. The physiologic process such as breathing pattern changes offered a teaching moment. However, the emotional and psychological, even spiritual, transition held greater impact.

Watching a beloved but troublemaker of a kid in his final hours with divorced parents on either side of the bed is something I'll never forget. I noticed the mom looking across the figurative chasm of the dying child at the father with such compassion, even love, for the grief she was unable to spare him. Then later, when the father could take no more, she witnessed her son's last moments. The parent who had brought her boy faithfully to clinic and hospital in-stays, who had been told the news of his tumor's recurrence, wept beautifully across him, declaring, "I loved him. I loved him."

I observed another gripping expression of a mother's love while watching a favorite patient die. She faithfully sat by his side as if on alert while the grandmother and father of the dear boy, their only child, wept and prayed with eyes closed. I watched in awe at this mother, who upon recognizing his long last drawn breath, stood quickly and tenderly kissed him upon the cheek as it slowly turned away from her to rest on the pillow beside him, "Bye, mijo." I allowed myself to grieve only later, as I watched the family trio from behind the nurses' station head toward the elevator for the last time with their bags in tow.

Years after my time spent at Santa Rosa Children's Hospital as a medical student, resident, and practicing physician, I returned for a visit with the pediatric hematology/oncology staff. It was late, and many of the nurses and doctors I had worked with had already left for the day; some had even retired from their positions after years of treating children in South Texas. I did manage to speak with Dr. Anne Marie Langevin. As my attending physician during my fourth-year rotation, she had played a pivotal role in my decision to pursue pediatric medicine. She was now the department chair. I also ran into a nurse I remembered as well. I had assisted her as a medical student while she accessed a beautiful little girl's port, preparing her for routine chemotherapy. The child's name was Bethlehem, and she was a survivor. We all reminisced about our experiences and recalled some of the patients' names. After leaving Dr. Langevin's office, I wandered back to the ward after saying goodbye to the staff in the clinic. The doors to the ward had been sealed with tape due to extensive reconstruction. I pushed through.

My footsteps echoed down long empty halls as I made my way through the ward, through the doors to the bone marrow transplant unit, now empty, after having served as administration offices for the past decade or so. I walked through the nurses' station—where we had gathered throughout the day, writing in charts, checking the computer for lab and test results—and finally down the hall, walking in and out of patient rooms. Peeling wallpaper borders remained, beds were empty and stripped, as were the floors and cabinets that once held medications and supplies. I didn't sense a tangible presence of the ghosts of children who had resided there, who had suffered and even died there, but the memories of them were palpable. The hemophiliacs' sudden return to character and laughter, once their pain was controlled, the un-burrowing from underneath her fluffy pillow, once Gabriella recovered from pancreatitis, the retching of Daniel that could be heard down the hall, parents sitting at the bedsides for endless hours, the slate of pre-teen boys we seemed to have lost within a few short years due to T-cell leukemia, the swinging IV poles on their way to the game room. They were no longer here. Silence. Emptiness.

The walls couldn't talk; they were never meant to, but the children's stories housed within those rooms for some time were absorbed and infused into the caretakers who showed up faithfully for work. They live on, inside of some of us who were privileged to have played a small part in their care, even as small as sharing a dance video, or as humbling as standing at the foot of a bed, witnessing a small life come full circle.

Chapter 10
Way Behind on *Rent*

When I was around ten or eleven years old, my mom and dad allowed me to accompany them to a live musical in Dallas, Texas. The show was *Auntie Mame,* featuring Juliet Prowse, and the venue was the Music Hall at Fair Park. My dad was more than a little self-conscious that there seemed to be no other children my age in attendance, but, much to Mom's credit, she knew I would love the singing and dancing without appreciating much of the adult humor. She was right. I was so mesmerized by the costumes, dancing, and revolving set changes with an open curtain, that I thought nothing of Mame's friend, Vera Charles, being hauled around by a group of male dancers over the heads of everyone during the opening party scene. The fact she was stoned drunk never crossed my mind. Nor did I think it inappropriate or out-of-place when Mame's single secretary, Agnes Gooch's stage entrances were greeted with enthusiastic laughter at the sight of her expanding waist-line and repeated references to her taking calcium. What I did appreciate was the magnificence of the setting and how the stage could transport me out of my chair into another realm for a little while, then leave me with the memory of its sounds and lights serenading me to sleep many nights afterward.

That 1970 excursion to Fair Park's Dallas Summer Musicals would not be my last. In fact, a yearly tradition of attending at least one of the shows in an offered series had begun for me; my parents had been attending since the days it began as an outdoor theater housed in the park's band shell. Over the years, through all the elegant renovations and changes the Music Hall underwent, I was privileged to see shows like *Annie Get Your Gun, The King and I, Chorus Line, Wonderful Town,* and others that featured the talents of Yul Brynner, Debbie Reynolds, Lauren Bacall, and Paul Lynde, to name a few. It was the closest I would get to Broadway for many years, but my memories couldn't have been fonder or richer. So, when my daughter voiced an interest in attending the Music Hall's special showing of *Rent* during the 2009 season, I was excited to return after a long hiatus from my favorite stage.

There had been a buzz about *Rent* ending its long, twelve-year run on Broadway and subsequently hitting the road for a national tour. In fact, there had been a buzz about *Rent* on the artistic radar for a long time, but it was something to which I paid little attention, other than planning to watch the movie version someday. Once I purchased the tickets, I purposely remained ignorant of the production's plot and content and showed up for the Saturday night's performance one May, ready to take it all in from the vantage point of fresh eyes. Clearly, from all the excitement and energy in the air exuding from an abundance of youth, I was about the only one in the place who hadn't seen or didn't know what *Rent* was about. I sat with my daughter in floor seating behind the season-ticket holder section, and, just before the actors took their places on stage, I started to read what all the fuss was about.

"*Rent*: An Unlikely Musical Milestone," by Mark Schumann was the feature article in the production's playbill and beautifully written, I might add. What left me tingling before the show ever started was the story behind the making of *Rent* and its subsequent place in Broadway history. Jonathan Larson, the young composer who worked tirelessly on the show's music and script for ten years while employed as a waiter at various New York restaurants, "would never celebrate the magic his musical created." After the final dress rehearsal before the off-Broadway opening, Mr. Larson returned to his walk-up flat, put on a pot of tea and died suddenly of an aneurysm that had not been previously diagnosed. The story of his death was the embodiment of what his musical projected about the "dark challenges" that artists living in the East Village in the 1980s faced daily: they were rent—torn apart. So, armed with my newfound knowledge about the composer and the musical's content regarding turbulent relationships, bad living conditions and the meal-to-meal existence of its characters, I sat back, ready to enjoy.

It's embarrassing even today to reveal that, after hearing the lines hauntingly sung to the show's first act, I still did not have a clue to the undertow all the characters were facing either directly or indirectly within the show. Charles Isherwood's article in the theater section of *The New York*

Times, "525,600 Minutes to Preserve" (September 17, 2008), said it beautifully:

"Just three questions set to a simple, mournful, gently shaped melody...
Will I lose my dignity?
Will someone care?
Will I wake tomorrow from this nightmare?
"You probably need to have lived among gay men coming of age during the years when AIDS became a global calamity to recognize just how much bone-deep knowledge of the specific terrors of the time is packed into those three little lines."

I thought the song had more to do with people living in a hopeless cycle of poverty; a single costume change would set me straight on that account.

In the second act, the flamboyant, dressed-in-drag character Angel, with the help of his partner, slowly enters from back stage left, wearing gauzy off-white pajamas. I didn't even need the silent weeping of the girl sitting next to me to indicate which direction we were heading. I may have been a newcomer to *Rent,* but I was certainly not green when it came to knowing the devastation wreaked by AIDS; my medical training in the early '90s had been marked by it.

• • • •

The third year of medical school consists of clinical rotations through the different specialties represented within the hospital and medical/surgical clinics. They typically last six to twelve weeks, including general and elective rotations, and are concluded with a test. The mother of these is considered by most to be *Medicine,* short for internal medicine rotation. Medical schools are typically located strategically to serve the less privileged and indigent population, while at the same time functioning as specialty referral centers. Hence, there is no shortage of patients with serious disorders and complications associated with a wide variety of disease processes. The medical training presents tons of information to absorb and hopefully retain, and many opportunities to apply book knowledge to real-life situations. The task of compiling all this information regarding patient status usually falls on the shoulders of the third- or fourth-year medical student of the team (headed by an attending physician, residents, intern, Pharm.D. student, in declining order). The basic role of the medical student is information gathering and reporting, which, in turn, can often involve the most direct patient contact. My first AIDS patient was an immediate introduction into the third-year general medicine stint.

He was a Hispanic male who appeared much younger than his chronological age of thirty-plus years. He sported a thick crop of black hair that matched the color of his eyes, which were never hostile or defensive. The first time I entered the four-bed ward to check on two of my assigned patients, he was sitting cross-legged in the bed across from my other patient, an older Hispanic male suffering from multiple diabetic complications. The younger HIV-infected patient was being treated for PCP (pneumocystis pneumonia), a potentially life-threatening infection that occurs in immunocompromised individuals. He was much improved from when he first entered the hospital and was listed as a routine check, which involved my reporting his vital signs and listening to his chest. Still, I had to go through his chart, learn about his past and present medical history and follow his course of treatment throughout the rest of my rotation.

For my first hands-on experience, I was not so much cautious as puzzled. Confused by a lifestyle I didn't understand, it was somewhat intimidating dealing with patients inhabited by a virus that crippled them with profound emaciation and weird infections: infections that were AIDS-defining by their very being, by just showing up on the culture or blood smear. If I seemed a little detached initially, it didn't take long for him to breach the gap.

I entered the ward one day to go over some important prognostic details with the elderly diabetic patient and his wife. Because the patient seemed to be deteriorating, the job of addressing in-hospital DNR (do not resuscitate) orders had been delegated to the third-year medical student: me. Neither the couple nor I spoke the same language, so I began to describe his medical condition and pending decisions in very loud and slow English. I was saved from floundering by my AIDS patient in the neighboring bed. He, without prompting, began to interpret the medical dialogue for the patient and consequently began to unravel some of the confusion. While facing his own plight, he weaved the Spanish dialogue with such compassion yet eloquent directness that I could discuss the seriousness of the other patient's medical trajectory far more efficiently and with greater understanding than if I had been on my own. From that day on, I related to my dark-eyed young friend a little differently, though he would be the one to ultimately qualify the change in me. The stigma of AIDS patients within the halls of the hospital and its ancillary clinics during the 1990s echoed much the same sentiment as that of the outside world.

During my third-year surgical rotation, the indignant moans from residents over having to take an AIDS patient into surgery, their callous remarks regarding "a bloodbath in there," verified a previous attitude suspected among other professionals during clinicals. My dermatology rotation was a cushy elective that teamed me with two upper-level residents, a dermatology intern and two other medical students. Our days were spent in clinic and consulting on hospital patients. One such patient we were asked to look in on was an AIDS patient with a case of scabies known as crusted (Norwegian) scabies. It is a severe form of scabies usually found in patients with weakened immune systems and is highly contagious because of the large number of mites and eggs contained within the crusting sores. Indeed, this patient's entire outer ear lobe was crusted over. Our senior resident was intent on getting a closer look during the examination, while the overzealous intern kept repeating words of caution: "Be careful! Be careful. Now, Sue, be careful." He might as well have had the patient ring a bell at the sound of our entering, declaring, "Unclean! Unclean!" The isolation rooms down the length of the infectious disease hall had much the same effect.

Just entering the room of an AIDS patient might entail downing a paper gown, face mask and a pair of rubber gloves in the vestibule before going in and promptly disposing of them in the designated receptacle before exiting. As isolating as it was behind two double-glass doors, those patients suffering from infections that trended outside the norm were victims of the kind of isolation that is born out of fear of the unknown. For instance, our otolaryngology team consulted on a man regarding a fungal infection that was causing his face to slide off his skull. He lay still and never opened his eyes but talked to us while we examined his throat, nose and ears, answering, "Yes, ma'am," "No, ma'am" and "Thank you, ma'am." On the other side of the glass window to his room, the nurses' station buzzed with activity, but the two beds beside him remained made and empty within the silent room. He was removed and alone.

Similarly, an emaciated man caught my eye upon entering the busy ICU ward inside the VA hospital. We locked eyes as I brought up the rear of our medical team rounding on one of our patients. I must have done a double take at the shell of a man sandwiched between two other patients against the wall. He rested upright against his pillows, his sallow complexion emphasized by the overhead light. His eyes never flinched as my face must have suddenly communicated my realization that he was a living person. As surprising as the appearance and pathology of this disease was, it remained foremost in our minds and topped many a list of *differential diagnoses.* No one was exempt from suspicion, for I had encountered my own day of thorough inquisition as a medical student.

During the hot summer between my first and second year of medical school, I became very ill after eating some apparently tainted food over the Fourth of July weekend. I naively decided to treat myself and borrowed some medication to stop the massive diarrhea I was experiencing—to prevent dehydration. But the plan backfired: I became more ill when the diarrhea stopped, for the infection simply incubated within me and revved up in my bloodstream. By the time a fellow medical student took me to the emergency room, my blood pressure dropped with vertical positioning due to my dehydrated state accompanied by fever and chills. I was given IV fluids, placed on a gurney and moved into the hall of the crowded emergency room to await a room on one of the hospital floors. After hours of lying on my back in a busy intersection of internal medicine and gynecological/obstetric patients, I was moved around the corner, where I was rounded on by the medical team to whose service I was to be admitted.

I was wheeled into a room where they began to take a medical history and perform an examination. The senior resident began a line of questioning regarding my sexual past and the number of sexual encounters over the previous years. I may have only been a first-year medical student, but I knew enough to know he was including HIV positivity/cryptosporidium-causing-diarrhea in his differential diagnosis. So, in front of an all-male medical team consisting of three medical residents and a third-year medical student, I began trying to think back on potential contacts and deciding just how much history I would share willingly.

After spending fourteen hours in the emergency room, providing two stool samples (they lost one) and answering the same set of questions for different shifts of medical personal, I was finally transferred to my hospital room after 9:00 p.m. My medical student friend entered my room the next morning with widened eyes behind a paper surgical face mask. "What the hell do you have?" he exclaimed. There was an *enteric precautions* sign posted on the door of my isolation room. I was sitting smack-dab in the middle of the infectious disease ward. Not until I gained enough strength to get up and walk around did I realize it. Gingerly making my way down the hall, I saw the numerous backs of men curled in fetal positions on their beds. Some of the doors had precautionary signs posted, and some of the rooms contained various shrines consisting of religious candles and pictures. Because it was summer, and most of my friends were not at school, I felt a touch of the loneliness that pervaded this hall. There were no visitors to speak of, particularly at night, and no activity or communication between the patients or rooms. The feeling was surreal and differed greatly from the experience gained from rounding on a different set of AIDS patients I would encounter over the next two years.

In my third and fourth years of medical school I was subjected to several pediatric rotations that placed me periodically on the eighth floor of the downtown children's hospital, where pediatric hematology and oncology patients were housed. In my third year, I usually trailed a pediatric resident on call. During my fourth year, my pediatric oncology elective entailed following patients on the in-patient service and in the bone marrow transplant unit. Within that period, one or two hemophiliac patients were always on the floor, being treated for complications from AIDS.

In the 1980s, an entire generation of hemophiliacs was infected with the HIV virus through contaminated blood products: primarily clotting Factors VIII and IX concentrates. Prior to donor surveys and use of viral inactivation procedures of factor concentrates in 1985, more than fifty percent of all persons with hemophilia contracted HIV during the '80s, many of them children. By the time I arrived on the hematology-oncology ward in 1992, these children suffering with hemophilia all had AIDS and were in the hospital for treatment of diseases/infections resulting from their immunocompromised state. Respiratory complications and pneumonia seemed to be the most prevalent.

One morning during my fourth-year rotation, an adolescent male hemophiliac/AIDS patient, well-known by the hematology staff, showed up on the floor complaining of a pneumothorax (collapsed lung—collection of air in the space around the lung, preventing its full expansion). The kid had coughed so hard that he was bent over and appeared a little spent from the effort of walking. "I think I popped a pneumo," he said matter-of-factly. The chest x-ray confirmed he had self-diagnosed his condition correctly. In fact, the consulting surgical team got a little tickled by the straight-forward claim made by the patient who apparently knew his body quite well. "Yeah, he popped one all right," they said, while staring at the impressive chest film. It was a little too typical of the hemophiliac patients being admitted regularly for treatment of their AIDS-related illnesses instead of blood factor transfusions.

When I arrived as a pediatric resident the following year, they were all gone. I never rotated on a pediatric hemophiliac patient with AIDS during my residency years; they had been wiped out. This was confirmed by some of the hematology/oncology nurses who attended the regional summer hematology camp for children. A sector of kids who had received tainted blood products from the early '80s until 1985 were simply not represented. It was like a swath of ground had been plowed up from the middle of a wheat field, the wide, gaping trail left as a reminder that something formidable had passed through.

Rent was definitely a reminder, a return down memory lane where many lay buried: memories and people. For days after returning from the stage show, I sat in front of the computer learning all I could about *Rent*: its composer, the history of the show, its performers, etc. For days, the music—as well as the faces and stories I had forgotten—went around in my head. Angel's death scene, powerfully choreographed on stage, orchestrated with movement and heat, symbolized the delusions associated with fever and chills that very sick patients may suffer. It reminded me of a good friend in medical school relating how her only beloved brother had died in the throes of AIDS. "My mother [who was a nurse], stood between my shaking brother in the bed and the nursing staff coming for more blood draws and firmly cried, 'You will not touch him again!'"

I remembered a young man in my third-year internal medicine rotation who had returned to his native city to die, like the prodigal son's returning home—except his family hadn't been around him in years and didn't really know what to do with him, his condition, or his insanely long list of medications. After staying home for a short while, he was readmitted to our service wrapped in the same comforter he had brought with him when he first came to the hospital, only now, delusional with AIDS dementia.

They flashed before my eyes one after the other: the man with the sliding face, alone; the patient with the tracheotomy motioning with his one finger to turn out the overhead light, please; the near-corpse staring at me from across the intensive care unit; and the patient who did pull-ups in his room, took in as many calories as he could, trying to maintain his strength and weight, praying in front of his candles and posters. Then, after three days, the dam broke: I wept and wept, grieving over them, grieving over the lost opportunities of maybe making a difference due to my naiveté and distance. Though the anguish did not clear, my head certainly did, for I saw him. There he was, my patient sitting cross-legged in the hospital bed, wearing gauzy off-white pajamas, a shock of black hair and dark eyes to match. After all these years, his gentle face was as clear and imposing as the first time I walked into his hospital room, and I had to ask myself some difficult questions.

Did I treat him with dignity?
Did I show that I cared?
Did I impart a sense of hope within his nightmare?

Certainly, he would be the one to answer these, better than I could. More importantly, was he still alive? Did he take his AZT and show up for his medical appointments? Did he find compassion and support within his family and community? Why couldn't I have been more receptive and consumed with this passion all those years ago?

I was way behind on *Rent,* the musical and what the title meant: "to be torn apart." A musical, nearly ten years in the making before its debut on

Broadway, addressed the "dark challenges of its characters living in New York City's East Village." I was also behind on connecting with my patients in a way that let them know I cared. I went into medicine with the intention of specializing in the treatment of cancer, inspired by the death of my best friend who suffered from Hodgkin's lymphoma. Though that goal morphed and changed over the course of medical school and residency, I had plenty of opportunities to walk around inside the skin of others suffering from various maladies and infirmities. I could have offered a little more of myself than learn what their bodies were teaching me. I don't think I took full advantage of that. I have no way of going back and asking my patients if I imparted healing—other than what their medical charts dictated—for some are no longer around to ask.

Chapter 11
Through the Back Door

Career transitions—or, in my case, career paucity—are always difficult to navigate. Such was the case in my fourth decade. I found myself at home raising two small children and taking care of the house after a long quest for a medical degree and completed residency in pediatrics. I had even practiced in a private pediatric office for some time, until a bout with major depression forced me to take a leave-of-absence from work. I, of course was grateful to my friend/employer, Dr. R. K. Johnson, for the much-needed time off with family and counseling to set my world somewhat straight again. I was also grateful to him for supporting the difficult decision I eventually made to leave the practice to spend an undetermined amount of time at home with my kids.

I took great pleasure in keeping the house and monitoring the kids' TV schedule: PBS in the mornings, Disney DVDs and children's PBS shows in the early evening. After so many years of schedules and deadlines, the task of making memories for my kids was a treat, whether it involved trips to the Hill Country, neighborhood kid play, or going in search of a "watering hole" during the hot San Antonio summers. It was a pain in the pocketbook for me to stop working, so, what we lacked in finances, we made up for in creative but simple ways to spend time. Pizza and a rented movie on a Saturday night became a big deal. Then, just like that, those mornings of walking the dog and baby, waiting for the bus to bring the pre-kinder home were over. I had a daughter in the first grade and an almost five-year-old son who loved spinning on his tire-horse swing, which hung directly over the spot in the backyard where he peed. My time was still filled, but I began to question when and where I would return to work. The fear of not being able to practice medicine again agitated me to the state of feeling unsure about myself and my intended purpose. *All that time and effort, for what?* The fact that my medical school loans demanded monthly attention didn't help matters either.

During this time, I happened upon a Bill Moyers documentary, *On Our Own Terms: Moyer on Dying*. The show was a four-part series on PBS, delving into the lives of patients and caregivers addressing very candidly their desires to die at home, pain-free, in the presence of and surrounded by family and those closest to them. The production was two years in the making, as Bill Moyer crossed the country visiting hospitals and hospices, as well the homes of those who shared their most intimate stories of living and dying. I didn't see all the episodes, but the one I caught addressed "What to Expect When Death Comes." It included an interview with Dr. Sean Morrison of Mt. Sinai School of Medicine, department of geriatrics and medicine. It was the first time I had heard the term *palliative care*. I was familiar with hospice; my best friend had been under the care of hospice for pain management due to advanced stage Hodgkin's lymphoma until her death. It was one of the reasons I had entered medical school; but I was unaware of the combined specialty palliative/hospice care. I was so moved by the program that I decided to look up the one person in San Antonio I associated with hospice: my instructor during an elective course my first year in medical school, Dr. Marion Primomo.

Before the days of Google, I picked up the gigantic San Antonio telephone book and started running down the line of hospices listed. I dialed number after number, asking if Dr. Primomo was there, until someone replied, "Let me put you on hold. I'll see if she's available." "She's still alive!" I gleefully yelled (while on hold, of course). Bless her heart; not only did Dr. Primomo spend a good fifteen minutes discussing the role of hospice with me; she kept trying to place me from our brief six-week class encounter. She extolled the Bill Moyer's program and told me, "There's no money in practicing hospice, but there will be someday," referring to the aging baby-boomer generation and their ongoing advocacy for end-of-life-care on "their terms." Just before we hung up, she asked me if I had heard about the pediatric palliative care program that Dr. Javier Kane had started recently at Santa Rosa Children's Hospital.

My recollection of Dr. Kane was brief. During my third year of residency, he was one of two new faculty members added to the pediatric hematology/oncology department. I had never been on a rotation with him or been on call when he was the attending physician in charge; however, I had seen him on the eighth floor. During my last stint in the pediatric intensive care unit, he had entered the facility to round on a patient and came upon one of the teams' patients' spiraling downward rapidly. After the patient was stabilized, I remember a brief conversation with him. Having a love for the oncology staff, I was glad to see two new faces added to their over-worked ranks. He was nice, cordial and spoke eloquent English with a Spanish accent due to his growing up in Monterrey, Mexico, with a Hispanic mother and an American father. I decided to give him a call. *What could it hurt?*

Our voicemail interchanges went something like this: First message: "Hello, Dr. Kane, I was a resident during your first year as an attending; I was interested in learning more about the pediatric palliative care program at Santa Rosa you've recently started. I am a board-certified pediatrician and have always had a passion for end-of-life care. When you have time, I was wondering if I could learn more about the program and see if there is training available at some point in the future for someone with my background. You can reach me best at this number..." Second message a couple of days later: "Hello, this is Dr. Kane; I am returning a call someone at this number left in regard to the pediatric palliative program. This is my direct line if you are still interested in speaking about this with me. I look forward to hearing from you." Before returning the call—*Oh, my God! It's Dr. Kane. He actually left me a message! Maybe this is not such a crazy idea!* Third call, in which we finally spoke: "Dr. Kane, hello, this is Sherry Scott. Yes, I had called earlier regarding your program that was brought to my attention by Dr. Primomo of San Antonio Hospice." "Uh, huh, could you tell me more about why you're interested and a little more about your background?" I proceeded to go through my medical training at the UTHSC at San Antonio, discuss my history of hospice involvement, my current unemployment situation, and my interest re-piqued by the Bill Moyer's documentary series. A profound silence followed. Then Dr. Kane, in that genteel Spanish accent, drawled, "I find it very interesting you are calling at this time."

Unbeknownst to me, the palliative program within the first six months of implementation had exceeded expectations of patient enrollment to the point of overtaxing Dr. Kane and the small staff assigned to him that included a program director and a patient care coordinator. He had, just the day before my initial phone call, said to the patient care coordinator RN, "I need some help." After establishing that I had kept my medical license up to date, Dr. Kane said he would get back with me. The next time we talked, he wondered if I could meet with him and Dr. Antonio Infante, whom at that time was the department head of the Pediatric Hematology and Oncology Division at the UTHSC at San Antonio.

Less than a week later, I was having lunch with the two physicians along with my husband and four-year-old son, Tyler. Their proposition was simple: they offered me a part-time position within the division that included joining Dr. Kane's team as an assistant professor in palliative care and overseeing the long-term cancer survivor clinic on the eighth floor. The offer was beyond what I had anticipated, but it did not come without some trepidation. Although Tyler was already in pre-kindergarten, I had not wanted to start back to work until he started kindergarten. The offer was too good to pass up, even if the timing seemed a little premature for my liking. It was settled. I was going back to work within the department I had always wanted to be—the very department that had been my reason for entering pediatric residency. Instead of stepping off the eighth-floor elevators as a hematology/oncology fellow, I was coming in through the back door as a palliative care pediatrician, interacting with the patients I enjoyed most.

Dr. Kane impressed upon me from the start the demographic details of the patient population we served. To Dr. Kane's surprise, after beginning the program within his own division, an overwhelming response came from physicians within the community who had patients with *special-care* needs. These kids had no medical home. In other words, kids who were severely developmentally delayed due to issues such as metabolic disturbances, postnatal infections, or birth trauma were cared for by many specialists regarding their body system of knowledge and training; however, no one seemed to be steering the ship and helping the family navigate the waters of continuing moments of crisis they would surely encounter due to complicated medical courses. These children were not necessarily going to die anytime soon, but they were certainly not curable and would face increasingly uphill battles before dying prematurely.

I began, armed with two handbooks Dr. Kane gave me on the first day: *Pain Management in Children with Cancer,* published by the Texas Cancer Council and *Primer of Palliative Care,* by Porter Storey, MD. I was welcomed by the team, Christie Torklidson, the program director, and Cindy Beckwith, RN, the patient care coordinator, as well as the ancillary staff, and all the attendings I had previously trained under during rotations on the eighth floor. Cindy had been holding down the fort under the direction of Dr. Kane, often running him down for prescription refills and his signature on orders, as the ever-increasing patient load began to stretch the two of them. I was here to help with that, if she would allow it.

The first time I went out on a home-patient visit with Cindy, she immediately let me know that she was perfectly capable of going it alone. After all, it had been her and Dr. Kane for the last year and a half, and she felt very comfortable with the responsibility. I had no doubt on that account, but I was eager and wanted to get out in the field for some hands-on-training. I don't remember the patient or the circumstances, but after hearing about her cheerleading daughter at Kansas State, previous nursing career and her opinion on why children should be allowed to die better in America, we were a hit. We were on the same page, and so a remarkable and ensuing partnership regarding the care of our slate of patients began.

What I thought would be a chance to get back into the halls of critical care, housed within the pediatric intensive care unit, turned out, not to be the heart of what I was after. Though we served the patients and families within the PICU (pediatric intensive care unit), at the request of the specialists who wanted to ensure families there were other options, our outpatient visits—those heart-to-heart talks with families that occurred within the intimacy of their homes—proved just as, if not more, fulfilling. Our continuing interaction with the patients in the hospital proved challenging, particularly when I had to write orders on the chart from a consultant viewpoint that would be read by my previous attendings. I discussed this dilemma with Dr. Kane, concerning my freshman-like status within the units, manned by physicians whose clinical experience far exceeded mine. Dr. Kane just laughed, "How do you think I felt, when I first wrote orders directed toward the likes of Dr. Thomas Mayes (Pediatric Department Chair and director of the PICU) or Dr. Mangos (Department Chair of Pediatric

Pulmonology), instructing them to 1) Touch the patient daily. 2) Turn on *Teletubbies*. 3) Aid the patient and the family to find meaning and purpose in the midst of suffering, etc." And so my journey began with a slate of patients and a team who relished the opportunity of offering hope along lines that diverged from mainstream care.

Several patients had been on the rolls for some time; our nurse coordinator had established ongoing relationships with the families to help facilitate them through tough decisions that certainly lay ahead for their loved ones. Even when nothing seemed to be pressing concerning care of the patient, the nurse coordinator made routine house visits and calls to maintain the connecting thread. Of course, the risk of becoming close—very close—to the patient and the family was part of the job, and our team took it seriously. After all, we were in it for the long haul: we understood that we would be attending children's funerals regularly and staying in touch with families after the deaths of their children. Cindy was excellent at advocating for her patients and, as the good and protective mother that she was to her own kids, she proved the same for our patients we discussed weekly in our team meeting. Her effort in many cases assured our team's pivotal role in guiding families through medical decisions on behalf of the patients; we were trusted if we had done our job well. One such case involved a girl referred to our team after she had endured a difficult and arduous PICU course surviving pneumonia and bacterial sepsis. *Surviving* was putting it lightly; it was not a plight that the medical staff or her out-patient physicians wanted her to have to go through again.

Ruby was one of five kids born to her petite mother. She was the third in line, but by far the favorite. Ruby was born with a chromosomal defect, Trisomy 18, also known as Edward Syndrome. It is a rare error in cell division in which an extra copy of the eighteenth chromosome exists. (The body has twenty-three pairs of chromosomes that carry genetic information from each parent.) Occurring 1 in 6,000 live births, it is potentially life-threatening in the early months and years of the child. In fact, fifty percent of babies carried to term with the chromosomal defect will be stillborn. There is a random occurrence of Mosaic Trisomy 18 (even rarer), where an extra chromosome is present in some but not all cells in the body; such was the case of Ruby. Typical characteristics found in these children include heart defects, kidney ailments, intestinal track abnormalities, esophageal defects, microcephaly (small cranium), low set ears, severe developmental delays. As a result, they are totally dependent on others for their basic survival needs. A small number of these children will live into their twenties or thirties, but with significant developmental delays as previously mentioned. Ruby turned eighteen years old just prior to her referral for a palliative care team assessment.

    The dynamics of the family were made immediately clear to us all. The mother overtly favored Ruby, was deeply devoted to her care (sometimes at the expense of excluding her other kids) and made it known that she herself would die the day Ruby died. Dysfunctional families encountered in the medical field, particularly when dealing with chronically ill children are common; in fact, they often become the norm. But this mom was so tied up in Ruby's plight she could not disassociate herself. Hence, our mission began. After leaving the hospital, Cindy made visits to the home periodically and got to know the mom and the siblings a little better, so much so that, when a respiratory illness landed Ruby in the hospital a year later, our team was immediately notified, and we made daily in-patient visits and charted recommendations as well; she did not go back into the PICU. Instead, Ruby and her family spent time in the Butterfly Room at the end of the eighth floor in Santa Rosa Children's Hospital.

    The Butterfly Room was the vision of Dr. Kane and some of the staff. The hospital renovated a room that was once inhabited by chaplain staff who ministered in the hospital. It was set up like a tiny apartment with an adjoining room and bath in addition to the room with the bed. An artist had painted the walls with beautiful murals of butterflies and other animals within their habitat of greenery and trees. The adjoining room had a sleeper couch and kitchenette with sink and microwave. This space gave families a quiet place to stay, uninterrupted, with patients during their final days and hours. Many families preferred this situation over hospice care provided in the home. Because many of these children had spent so much time at Santa Rosa, they desired the presence of some of the medical staff with whom they were familiar. No monitors were present and no vital signs were taken; rather, the nursing staff practiced a supportive model, overseen by our team who facilitated the management of pain—physical, emotional or spiritual.

I first met Ruby and her family during this admission. I sat patiently, sometimes twisting my wedding ring round and round to stay awake, while Dr. Kane spoke for long periods of time with the mom in Spanish. I couldn't understand what precisely was being said, though Dr. Kane would clarify later. Nevertheless, I appreciated the sincerity and seriousness of these encounters, particularly once when Dr. Kane actually kneeled to speak more directly with Ruby's mom, who sat in a chair, despondent with grief. We really didn't know which way Ruby would swing physically, because she had developed a paralytic ileus (blockage symptoms associated with lack of "peristalsis" or movement in the intestines that does not have a physical obstruction as the cause), associated with her respiratory illness. Many patients in already chronic compromised states can take a turn for the worse the longer their hospital course runs. Ruby did however recover and become stable enough to return home with her mother and the assistance of her previous home-health care provider. But it had been a setback—she did not regain the function she had before the respiratory insult.

As with any crisis or medical setback our patients endured, it provided our team the opportunity to sit down with the family and discuss difficult topics regarding the future care of their child. These setbacks typically resulted in a lessening level of function than before and often served notice of future complications for the patient. DNR orders, bargaining over medical measures to discard in favor of different ones that concentrated more on the quality of life rather than quantity were examples of topics that we discussed gently with the family. We, as a medical team, wanted not only to encourage the family to make decisions on behalf of their loved one but to grant them permission to make extremely difficult decisions that were ethically, medically and legally appropriate but were not in the curative vein of medicine. We wanted to make sure the family knew about other options and that they had a voice in choosing.

Ruby was now at that place, where her function and overall well-being had dropped. Our team stepped up visits to offer support and help facilitate a quality/comfort care approach to managing her. The privilege of being allowed to enter patients' homes and be invited into their inner sanctum was something I took seriously, and, one day after receiving a call from her mom, I made a home-visit to assess Ruby's respiratory status. After examining her,

I sat down on the bed and talked with her mother regarding the "crackles" in her chest I heard through my stethoscope. I assessed that she was not in any respiratory distress but might be coming down with something. I advised Mom to continue the same respiratory care and to contact us if any rapid changes occurred. More importantly, we began to talk about *her* overall status: How was *she*? How did *she* see Ruby?

In broken English and with the help of her oldest daughter, she conceded Ruby was not happy anymore, not like she had once been. She wasn't the same.

In the past, when her home-health nurse or her respiratory therapist would come and work with her—make her sit up and engage in her respiratory toilet (treatments that are designed to help clear mucous and secretions from the trachea and bronchial tree), Ruby would laugh and clap her hands. She liked music and would sing along, in her own indecipherable way. She loved her respiratory therapist, who was pretty "rough" with her, according to the older sister, but Ruby always playfully engaged with him. Now, she no longer laughed or seemed to care; she never clapped her hands anymore. I began to reiterate with her mom what we had discussed in the hospital. Now was the time to focus on keeping Ruby comfortable rather than proceeding toward painful invasive care. She was ready to listen and knew we had Ruby's best interest at heart. The goal of care was to keep Ruby comfortable in the presence of her family at home. I started her on a very small dose of morphine sometime shortly after this discussion, mindful that she had been previously administered many analgesic combinations while undergoing multiple lengthy PICU stays.

I wrote out the script to their preferred pharmacy with detailed instructions on dosage and time interval administration of the drug after an in-depth discussion with Ruby's mom. All were in agreement, but I neglected to request that the pharmacist directly go over the administration of the drug, or that the pharmacy provide a tiny syringe to deliver the analgesic, since it was a tiny dose. I had noted plastic syringes in the house the family were using for administering other meds, but they were larger than what would be helpful in delivering a one-milliliter dose instead of a ten-milliliter dose. I thought about it, left it up to the pharmacist, and, in retrospect, inadvertently set up the rest of Ruby's course that was not anticipated, but nevertheless assured her a palliative-care advocated approach to her care, right up to the end.

The following Saturday night, I received an urgent call from one of the daughters: Ruby was in trouble. In the background, I could hear her mother speaking frantically, along with the hurried excitement of others. Ruby wasn't breathing right and her response level was diminished. I said I'd be right over, and, just before I hung up, I made sure they had her outpatient DNR on hand. (We always recommended to families that they tape the document on the wall over the patient's bed.) I jumped in the car wearing raggedy shorts and t-shirt, sporting flip-flops and my hair in a mess. I sped the wrong way through the apartment complex gate—it's a wonder my tires weren't slashed by the blades in the exit-gate grate. When I pulled up in front of her door, the ambulance was already there.

I entered the small apartment, yelling, "Do not intubate her! She's a DNR!" The apartment was darker than usual, because the tiny hallway to the bedrooms was blocked by four gigantic male paramedics. In unison, they turned and looked at me, expressing, *Who the hell are you?* Of course, my appearance probably had as much to do with their incredulous looks as did my words. Once I introduced myself as her doctor, they immediately relaxed, and actually looked relieved.

To be fair, codes involving children are some of the most anxiety-provoking, gut-wrenching emergencies in medicine, and tension runs sky-high. General paramedics more routinely attend codes in adults rather than children—the relevant unfamiliarity adds to the uneasiness, as well as the fact that the patient is a child.

They asked if it were okay to give her Narcan to reverse the effects of the morphine. (Narcan, brand name for naloxone, is an opioid antagonist that is used in opioid overdose when respiratory depression occurs.) Just as I had feared on my drive over, Ruby had been given an incorrect dose. The mother had used a syringe on-hand and inadvertently delivered ten times the prescribed dose. However, because Ruby had been exposed to so many analgesics during her prolonged intensive care stays, the mistake hadn't proved fatal, and one shot of Narcan restored her to normal consciousness. Her respiratory status was still compromised due to her overall failing health; she was end-stage. So, we decided to load her up, and take her to the place that knew her best—Santa Rosa Children's.

I climbed in the back of the ambulance with Ruby and two paramedics, with the family following in two cars. Following so closely, in fact, that the ambulance driver stopped at one of the intersections and told them in a friendly manner to back off just a little. He was afraid they were endangering themselves and others by speeding through red lights to stay right behind us. We didn't have the lights on or siren; we were just headed to the hospital. I called ahead to the emergency room and reported her status to the physician and why we were coming; I wanted her admitted to the eighth floor.

The staff was anticipating her arrival and eagerly rushed us in, as with all cases arriving in an ambulance at a pediatric emergency department. The transfer to the eighth floor was already in progress. The physician asked if I would agree to their establishing venous access so that an IV drip of naloxone might be readily available, if the previous dose of Narcan wore off, and she quickly deteriorated into respiratory distress again. I agreed to the plan but told the nurse, "You've got one shot at it; we're not sticking her repeatedly. If you don't get it, we're going upstairs without an IV." If I did anything for Ruby that night, it was advocating for no more needle sticks. The nurse didn't hit the vein on the first try, so we proceeded to the eighth floor, where the oncology nurses under the direction of Dr. Kane and our team were waiting.

Ruby, like most of our "special needs" patients had a g-tube in place. (A gastrostomy tube is surgically inserted through the abdominal wall to deliver nutrition, liquids and/or medication into the stomach.) Many children, born with errors of metabolism, congenital abnormalities or suffering from events occurring during the neonatal period—such as infections or hemodynamic crises—are left with neurological deficits. These deficits can leave children with inability to swallow properly or even suck. Other entities, such as cystic fibrosis, demand such energy on the part of the patients to maintain adequate oxygenation that they have difficulty meeting their caloric needs for growth and development. The g-tube can deliver nutritional supplement in many children who may lead a pretty normal lives in other respects apart from their underlying condition. Such is not the case in end-stage adult diagnoses such as Alzheimer's: the placement of a g-tube does not promote relational or functional return but merely prolongs suffering and extends the dying process. Ruby's g-tube allowed us to deliver her analgesic medication through another route other than an IV or injection; or so we thought.

Throughout the next twenty-four hours, we could not get Ruby comfortable. We had her on a non-re-breathable facemask, which delivered the maximum amount of oxygen possible without a more invasive means, and scheduled doses of analgesics alongside an anti-anxiety medication, to assure her comfort level and sense of ease. One of the nurses on the floor reported that, after administering Ruby's drugs through the g-tube, she had to cap it off quickly, or the medicine would come right back out. Ruby's body was shutting down exactly how it had during her previous hospital stay for treatment of respiratory distress: she had developed another paralytic ileus. She was not absorbing any of the medication. We decided on another route of administration—we would dose her through her rectum.

The rectum is essentially the end of the gastrointestinal tract before it empties into the anal canal. It is primarily a reservoir for fecal contents but because of its plexus of veins that eventually drain back into major veins in the body, it can be used to administer medications, and even fluids for rehydration. Because the absorption level of medications can be erratic, and obtaining peak therapeutic drug levels take longer, it is not recommended for dosing acute pain management. Yet, for our purpose, it worked beautifully. As soon as we finalized the dosage and schedule, we had Ruby in a comfortable, relaxed state, and the same could be said for the family and staff. Ruby could then get on with the business at hand: dying in peace.

As the second day in the hospital drew on, everyone was getting prepared for the inevitable. Our nurse, Cindy, was already engaged with the older sisters in speaking with the funeral home and discussing details that the mom had not addressed: a dress for Ruby, financial cost, ceremony. The immediate family was gathering in the room, all except Ruby's younger brother and sister. Earlier in the day, while I was in the room visiting with the mom and checking on Ruby, Dr. Kane had stuck his head in the door. He spoke in Spanish to the mom. His words to her consisted of strongly recommending taking off the oxygen mask, because it would only prolong the dying process, and Ruby could go on all day like this. I thought, *"Wow."* I would not have had the courage to propose that plan to Mom, particularly given her fragile grieving state and her previous history of depression tied to Ruby's failing health.

By mid-afternoon, it was nearly standing-room-only surrounding Ruby's bed. Cindy, Dr. Kane and I, in addition to family members, remained in an attitude of silent prayer or within the silence itself. The sunshine outside the eighth-floor window filtered through the mini blinds, bathing the room in light as Ruby's breath came in long, slow drags. Dr. Kane stood against the wall next to Ruby's uncle, her mom's closest brother (who would die unexpectedly some months later). Ruby's mother was at the bedside, flanked by her two older daughters. Cindy and I sat on opposite sides of the foot of the bed. Then something happened that none of us would have predicted. I watched the mom, without speaking a word, slip the oxygen mask off Ruby's face and lay it to the side. She then sat Ruby up and folded her arms about her own neck, gesturing to her daughters to hold them there in place, because Ruby would not have the strength. Ruby was resting on her mother's chest. She was giving her permission to die; she was helping her die.

In all my experiences watching patients and their families interact, I had never witnessed such a selfless act. Then it hit me. I was bowed forward against Cindy's back when an adrenaline rush washed over me. My heart began to pound against my rib cage; I flushed from the top of my head down as my heart rate sped up, and I knew. I knew Ruby was passing, even though I couldn't see her. It felt like the scene from Steven Spielberg's *Empire of the Sun*, when Jamie, a prisoner of war in a Japanese internment camp during World War II, witnesses the death of a fellow prisoner upon the camp's evacuation. The young boy lies down beside the dying Mrs. Victor and is sure he sees her soul flying to heaven when he sees a flash on the horizon. Young Jamie actually witnesses the atomic bombing of Nagasaki, hundreds of miles away, but his interpretation of the moment transcends the physical world around him.

I patted Cindy on the back and whispered, "Way to go, Ruby." Her sister looked at me to see if she was gone. I nodded yes. Though I still couldn't see her, I knew she was. Later, at the nurses' station while we sat around discussing the events, I told Dr. Kane what had happened to me. He responded immediately, "I saw that; I saw your whole being flush." I would experience that same adrenaline rush several more times when dealing with patients, even a friend, nearing their times of death.

More Rubys were to come. Oh, not little girls with Trisomy 18, but kids of all shapes and sizes and disorders who would need us. They would leave before their parents were ready; they would need us to help them leave, to help their parents say goodbye, even though they lacked the voice to give them permission. Such was life in the world of pediatric palliative care; our contacts and experiences were vast within the realm of medicine and all that life could throw at young bodies and those they called family. We entered the world of osteosarcomas, cystic fibrosis, neurological devastation that lingered beyond neonatal infections and difficult deliveries, medulloblastomas, leukemias, ataxia telangiectasia, sympathetic muscular atrophy—even those disorders without a definitive diagnosis. As academically stimulating these pathologies proved to be, faces were attached to them. The *kids* kept us coming back; they kept us walking through the doors of the ICU and hospital rooms. The people they called family kept us entering their homes and following them into the sanctuaries of their parishes and places of worship, even out to the pauper cemetery where we said our last goodbyes. They are too many to recount individually, but they live on in the patient files, compiled literature, in the minds and souls of those who cared for them.

• • • •

Years after leaving my position within the department of oncology and hematology and moving from San Antonio, I still stay connected with our palliative care team members. Occasionally, I'll get an unexpected call from Cindy. It goes something like this: "Guess who just died?" Coming from anyone else, this would seem bizarre, particularly when noting the near-excitement in her voice, but, remembering how Cindy stayed on top of our patients and their families, it is not odd. It sounds perfectly normal, like we're about to walk through the door of the Butterfly Room together. To this day, Cindy regularly checks the newspaper obituary column to see if any of "our kids" are listed. The habit used to be to check for the listing of our consult patients, so we could be sure to send a card, or save the clipping and picture for our team. Now, I'm sure the habit continues, though I wouldn't be surprised if she rings up the family or sends a card on her own accord.

In phone calls like these, we marvel that one of "our kids" lived this long, particularly considering the burden of disease and disability they have carried for so long. We feel reconnected upon hearing the child's name. We return once again to days of team meetings, home visits, phone calls and funerals. It's a moment of bittersweet pain: sad to think they've suffered this long, joyful to know they are free at last—so very, very thankful we were given the privilege of knowing them.

Chapter 12
Coming Full Circle

Some aspects of human relations remain constant, even if we, personally, willfully change or allow ourselves to be changed by time's relentless hold over us, its rhythmic pulse as sure as the evening breaking tide. For example, family remains family whether we agree with each other, or vice versa; whether we understand and/or accept one another, or the opposite. Some people in our lives will never like us despite our best intentions and will exercise their power to humiliate or demonstrate their dislike toward us, either by their power of position or skill of manipulation and tomfoolery. As far as the people who really liked me or treated me well, I can't truthfully say I earned that affinity or blessing. But, I learned I could count on it from those who never wavered in their belief in me.

Perhaps because I'm female, I more readily identify the women in my life who either acted as a thorn in my side or who loved me through no fault or good of my own. Out of all the women I count dear, I can honestly say only a few *got me,* or truly knew me. And as time passing seems to shed a truer light, I find myself struggling with the same task, understanding myself. Even so, the paths of some I've known have crossed in unforeseeable ways—ways unexpected to them or me. Because they did, I'm left with a sense of wonder how our connectedness comes to be. We thrive long after their days have passed and go on remembering them for the good or bad.

My earliest memory of my mother's oldest sister, Aunt Mary, pertained to a gift she gave, rather than actual visual of her. Vintage Barbie Ponytail Dolls were first introduced in 1959, and the same style with slight changes ran through 1964. Judging by description, mine had to be the 1961 model, which would have put me at two years old that Christmas (typical gift from someone who never had or would never have children). I held the brunette beauty with her red lips, that black and white striped swimsuit and those black open-toe heels long before I could articulate sexy. Although I can't recall opening her for the first time, I remember the thrill of that cardboard single box that contained her and the inside flap door that tempted me with all the illustrations of latest Barbie fashions. Glimpses of that Christmas are more imagined than real, because memories of the house are indelibly imprinted on my past as much as the woman who lived there.

Whenever I watch the original movie production of *Miracle on 34th Street*, released in 1947, I feel an immediate connection to the Manhattan apartment of the young divorcée mother, Doris Walker, played by the beautiful Maureen O'Hara. The audience is first introduced to the apartment, during Macy's Thanksgiving parade, as Ms. Walker's second-grade daughter, Susan, played by a young Natalie Wood firmly gives her opinion of the store's Santa Claus upon her mother's return from her duties at Macy's. It was the compactness, the organized classic replica of my aunt's house. But my Aunt Mary didn't live in an apartment; she lived in a two-bedroom 1930s bungalow in the South Oak Cliff neighborhood of Dallas, Texas. The other connection was obvious; my aunt was a divorcée like Maureen O'Hara's character, during a time when *divorce* ostracized women, not unlike the "scarlet letter" of Hawthorne's 1850 novel. Because she didn't drive but took the city bus to her job at Baylor Medical Center, she embodied the life of a professional working woman of the middle class, making her way in the big city—even though Dallas in the 1960s was not the metropolis of Manhattan.

Her house sat in the middle of the block on Mentor Avenue, just up the street from the Veterans Administration hospital, opened in 1940 and located on Lancaster Street. I could see the original five-story brick and stone main building of the hospital if I stood in the middle of Mentor looking east. Next to it stood the modern multi-storied orange bricked hospital, built in 1967. Patients there were treated primarily for chronic diseases, although general and neurological surgeries were performed in the opening years. It was intimidating as hell. I pictured bloody gory bodies being delivered to its emergency room when sirens rang in the night. Tucked down in the covers of some makeshift bed in her living room, I was certain victims of car wrecks were on their way to be stitched back together, though the sirens were more likely from a police patrol car on the south side of Dallas or for a heart attack victim en route.

Up the front steps and enter: the living room with a big bay window shadowed by the white and forest green striped metal awning outside. An immediate left led to the compact kitchen with a table shoved up against the wall housing her two wooden chairs with blue vinyl covered seats, bathed in the light coming in underneath the matching white and forest green accented metal awning covering her kitchen window. Her kitchen door led out to the side of the house onto the drive with a strip of green grass down the middle. From the living room, exit into the hall that stretched between two bedrooms—the west one, containing my aunt's bedroom set; the east room, housing the Duncan Phyfe cherry-wood stained guest bedroom set. The linen cupboard located in the wall was just outside the pink bathroom at the east end of the hall: sink, bath-tub, wall space heater, and, on the wall, painted ceramic butterflies, whose base color revealed white wings rather than ivory, once decades of cigarette smoke were washed away after her death.

The delights that small house afforded my younger self, like the Pepsi-Cola salt and pepper shakers always on the kitchen table evoked memories of a different time—for she was different as well. She exuded the Hollywood era of the 1940s, not because she was notably beautiful or elegant, but rather carried that Lauren Bacall independent aura; the same swept hairstyle and slim figure didn't hurt either. The fact she chronically smoked Benson and Hedges without a filter, talked incessantly and wore red lipstick attributed to the glam image as well. But, I think it was more the divorced-single-independent-working-woman persona that held for me, the movie screen image. She was a very tender person, but difficult times had forced independence on her.

She was born Mary Ellen Farnsworth, 1912, in the small Texas town of Chambersville, first of my grandmother's six children. My grandmother was widowed when Aunt Mary and her sister, Marguarite, were school-age girls. She remarried a farmer, Alfred Henry Fletcher Taylor, with whom she had four more children, the last being my mother. My mother, seventeen years younger, never thought of Aunt Mary as a half-sister, and the same could be said of my aunt, even though she went to live and complete her education with grandparents on her father's side of the family. Times were tough on farmers; there was one less mouth to feed. My aunt flourished under the devotion of her paternal grandmother and was afforded a more *genteel* upbringing, comparatively speaking, than the rest of her siblings. Shortly after high school, she left for Draughan's Business College in Dallas, Texas, thirty miles north of the small community where she had grown up.

She married Uncle Raymond sometime after her education, while working in Dallas. The couple settled in the South Oak Cliff neighborhood while making their living as wholesale distributors of costume jewelry and ladies fine hosiery. Their business took them all around the country—primarily back and forth to California.

My memories intercept the couple at the tail-end of their marriage in the early '60s. Judging by early Christmas pictures, he's "in the picture," but I remember more my *divorced* aunt from Dallas, who visits my grandmother sometimes and always brings me cool gifts. Treasured visits to her house on the south side of Dallas always included my dad's complaints about having to drive "all the way across Dallas" and turning off the radio so he could negotiate the traffic. Once inside her bungalow, I was immediately drawn to the coffee table in front of the couch that housed a menagerie of painted china dogs in all shapes and sizes on a shelf just under the glass tabletop. Her collection of larger painted china dogs perched in the window sill next to the window air-conditioning unit and her stereo hi-fi.

She works at Baylor Medical Center on the south side of Dallas where she takes the bus to and from. She collects stamps, knows everything there is to know about Dallas, roots for the Dallas Cowboys and takes a trip to Disney World. She brings me back a gold filigree necklace with Tinkerbelle perched inside the pendant's golden hoop and promises to take me there when I turn twelve years old. But some distractions happen along the way that derails the coveted trip of a lifetime—for me anyway. While walking to the bus stop one morning on her way to work, she slips on the ice and cracks her pelvis. While recuperating in the hospital where she is employed, Uncle Raymond re-enters the picture when he hears the news of her unfortunate fall.

I remember sitting in our car outside the front of the hospital, what is now considered the old part of Baylor Medical Center on Gaston Avenue. Children weren't allowed past the first floor, so I was relegated to spending time in the pink marbled foyer. Upon our leaving, my dad spotted Uncle Raymond coming up the sidewalk in the rearview mirror. "Boy, Raymond sure has aged," my dad said, as I turned in my seat and spotted a short, stout man with salt and pepper hair wearing a suit. It was the first time I ever laid eyes on him and had cognition enough to remember it. As I watched him walk toward the hospital I thought he had a refined air about him. Apparently my aunt had thought so as well, once upon a time.

Raymond remained in the picture up until my junior year of high school. Shortly after that hospitalization, he and my aunt remarried. Apparently, the adults in the family were a little dismayed. My older cousin recalled a conversation between her parents after receiving the call from Aunt Mary regarding the nuptials. Her mother was aghast, "What could she be thinking?" and my uncle (my mother's oldest brother) responded, "I don't know what she's thinking, but she's gonna do what she's gonna do."

It turned out that my uncle was not at all "sophisticated." I don't ever recall seeing him in a suit again; though, his hair did get grayer. I found out years later that the fuss over my aunt remarrying had to do with Uncle Ray's lifestyle choices. Womanizing associated with strong drink apparently had played a significant part in their marriage breakup, but these things were never discussed. My kid-level understanding was: Raymond spun a lot of tall tales, tended to brag and his work ethic was somewhat questionable. Even so, I remember how they doted on one another, his big laugh, and when he was asleep in his chair to be careful not to wake him suddenly. After his retirement, they were always together in their home on Mentor Avenue, well after the neighborhood had significantly changed from the "white flight" that took place in South Dallas during the '60s.

When I was sixteen or seventeen, we got a call one night. Uncle Ray had been shot and killed at a neighborhood gas station. My aunt was alone in her home except for her longtime neighbor from across the street, "Mamie," who intended to sit with Miss Mary until her family came. My dad was adamant about leaving quickly, so I spent the night with a friend around the corner, as my parents made a hurried, middle-of-the-night drive to Dallas.

An altercation had taken place outside a neighborhood gas station while Uncle Ray was putting gas in his car after returning from fishing. Raymond had a couple of beers on board and became argumentative with the owner of the gas station. He angrily reached into his fishing vest for "something" and was shot in the chest. It had been some kind of "air pump," I was told later. *Bang.* He was gone.

I sometimes wonder now why at the time I didn't ask more questions about the incident, why nobody seemed that alarmed or surprised, why there was no investigation over a homicide that was ruled self-defense on the spot. I guess I was too wrapped up in my own interests to give it much thought, and no one else seemed that upset over it. My mom revealed to me many years later just what a "rascal" Ray was.

If he had been fishing, it had been before he went over to visit his lady friend around the block. He had had more than a "couple of beers on board": he was drunk and belligerent. Living in South Oak Cliff during the 1970s meant a poor minority neighborhood, and the fact that my white uncle had to have been in his late sixties: overweight, graying and without substantial income, this "relationship on the side" was more likely the result of liquor and bad business. So, of course, when this was finally revealed, I understood why nobody made a fuss. My aunt didn't even seem to grieve; not that I saw anyway. But then I wasn't around all that much; I knew that things were back like I remembered as a kid: my aunt was living independently in the middle of a South Dallas neighborhood with a bad reputation.

She remained defiantly independent until one day, while walking to the corner store where she bought small staple goods, she was attacked by a black teenage boy. They struggled briefly over her handbag in a game of tug-of-war until in exasperation she tersely said between gritted teeth, "Let go, you damn fool!" The young kid immediately dropped his grip and ran like hell. My mother was aghast at the news, saying, "Don't you realize you could have been hurt?" My aunt was adamant about defending her purse; after all, it contained her house keys and her social security card.

Well, life went on as usual for some years. She let her neighbors pick up small things for her at the market if they were going that way and carpooled with them to the larger grocery store twice a month to fill her longer shopping list. We visited occasionally. She went with us to the Dallas Summer Musicals in Fair Park, continued to supplement her small social security check with her stamp collecting/trading and occasionally visited us by way of the Trailways bus. But one day during a surprise visit I made while traveling through Dallas on my way back from seeing a friend, I discovered a radical change in my aunt.

It was the summer of 1980 on a sunny Sunday afternoon. I sat in her kitchen on her metal step stool while she rustled up something for me to eat. She wore a soft pink '50s-style cotton dress and served me crackers with a bowl of celery soup, which was surprisingly good. I've not forgotten it, or the way she was dressed—perhaps because I hadn't seen her in an everyday dress before, only casual slacks. It made her look younger, and even more like Lauren Bacall. Perhaps, because she was in love.

She talked incessantly (which she was known for anyway) about a yard man named Bill. "Now, he's not a handsome man, but he's a nice man. He is very humble and soft spoken, not a braggart at all like your Uncle Ray." Well, apparently, he had shown up one day to trim some trees, and she had taken him something to drink, iced tea or such, because it was so hot. He admirably noted that she liked to talk but hadn't invited him inside the house. How she managed to have repeated contact with him, I can't remember, but the talk was all about this elderly man who had been shipped off as a young GI in World War II. The fact that he wasn't at all like Raymond seemed to lighten her feet as she flitted around that small kitchen like a schoolgirl.

My mother brought up the subject one day with a smile, "Well, I think it's nice she has found a friend." "Mom," I countered, "this is no friend. She's in love with him. I know; I saw her." By November, she was wearing a little gold wedding band set, with a small diamond, after he had whisked her off to the justice of the peace. And all was right with the world for a time.

They both acted like kids in love for the first time. I recall a conversation in which my dad exclaimed how embarrassed he was over their open display of affection, "Seventy-year-olds acting like kids!" "Oh, I think it's nice," Mom said, "my husband never kisses me in public." "My wife never kisses me either!" said my dad, followed by Mom's laughter.

The kisses and road trips, sitting together, holding hands and days of bliss spent on Mentor Avenue happened right up till the last kiss he gave her. A Hispanic man with his young son who did their yard work (replacing Bill because he was older and now married to the woman of the house) invited Bill for an afternoon of fishing in their small boat. He was so excited! According to my aunt, he literally skipped down the front walk on his way to the waiting truck, before returning to the front porch to get one more kiss from her for good luck. The afternoon turned sad for the fishing trio. Bill had a catastrophic heart attack while in the boat, and his fishing friend, with his young son in tow, had to rush him to the nearest hospital. He was admitted to the cardiac intensive care unit after a procedure to stabilize him was performed.

My aunt was home, happily experimenting with decoupage when she received the news at her door. The man and his son had come back. They delivered her to the hospital. Bill stayed in the unit for a couple of days on the ventilator, but I could tell by the language from the cardiologist that it was only a matter of time before his inevitable demise. I was only a college student in pre-med studies at the time, but I remember sitting in the waiting room with the family on another Sunday afternoon, feeling for this Northeastern-bred cardiologist. He was trying his best to describe the gravity of the situation while my aunt graciously thanked him for all he was doing. Not one to let anyone get away without a full-fledged conversation about how much she loved Bill, their history together and what he meant to her, she looked up at the doctor standing over her and earnestly said, "These have been the best seven years of my life. He has been so good to me." I struggled with the tears in my eyes, and I watched this physician struggle with his own emotions and response—the long-standing condition of Bill's heart was obviously out of his hands.

Life went on for my aunt, but she was different this time. She harbored herself in her house and didn't come to see us much anymore. She repeatedly turned down offers to come at Christmas, and, with increasing age, she became more irritable and less fun. She did, however, continue to go out to eat with us when we would visit but became pickier about where she would go. She still talked incessantly but less animatedly, as she droned on about something. I can remember watching in agony, as I waited for what seemed like an eternity for her to finish a bowl of fruit at Luby's Cafeteria, because she kept talking between bites. I thought she would never finish that plum!

I knew that, one day, I would stop sending Christmas cards to her home, stop having to make detours off Interstate 35 on my six- and seven-hour trips between South and North Texas to drop in and visit, but I didn't think her pending death would bring her back to the small town where I was raised.

I didn't imagine that her last days would cross paths with another woman whom I remembered just as much for the unfair way she treated me as for the role she played in my young life.

Everyone's had a bad year in school, possibly more than just one. It's safe to wager that the bad year remembered as such involves a bad teacher or one known for unfair treatment. Sometimes, it's hard to know which it is: bad teacher or bad experience. But when it happens over and over to you and you alone, well, you begin to think, "They're out to get me." My fifth-grade year and the teacher who emblazoned the damn thing in my memory forever was *out to get me!*

She was a fearsome sight. In 1970, aging teachers who expected to stick it out until their retirement were not exceptions—they were the rule. It wasn't so much that she was older, it was the way she wore her *older*. Her standard of appearance was dyed coal-black hair that hung to her shoulder in coiffed waves, powdered face that whitened her entire countenance (save for the bright red lips that continued to be so throughout the day), and long-waisted, swinging jersey-print dresses that hung just below the knees, above her two-inch pumps. Yet, her cold black eyes that often blazed underneath her brooding black eyebrows sealed the deal as one scary teacher, whose very name—read aloud by your mom, announcing with whom you would be spending the entire year—held a certain dread. My immediate reaction, "Oh, no!" proved to be correct. I even recall the car she drove (as opposed to the cars of any other schoolteacher I ever had), so accustomed I was to looking for it in the parking lot while walking up to school. I could spot it anywhere, and did so many years later, well after completing the fifth grade. Just the sight of it brought a familiar chill.

I did not get off to a bad start. It was just... well, she was mean, and I seemed to be an easy target. The fact that the class favorite had it in for me at different times throughout the school year didn't help matters either.

Lesa lived across the street from my family for a short time. She was a tall girl with long blonde, perfectly straight hair. Her father was higher up in the company where my dad worked. One day, while walking around his work station, I asked my dad why Mr. Woods had a bigger desk than his. My dad responded, "That's what that college education will do for you." The fact that her dad had a higher position may have played a part in our antagonistic relationship, but it was milked quite frequently by a mutual friend of ours.

A petite girl with dark hair and eyes, Denise had her popularity handed down to her, compliments of her two older siblings and the known position of her dad: head coach of the town's university football team. Having been separated from her fourth-grade *other* short friend, two-peas-in-a-pod Terry, Denise set herself up as the favorite friend in a tug-of-war between Lesa and me. And she was brilliant at it. One week, I was the best friend, invited over for a Friday night sleepover, invited to sit with her at lunch and in choir and to run with her during recess. The next week, she abruptly dumped my company for Lesa's. While I sat dejected in choir class, the two girls whispered and gloated, until Denise rang my phone the following week, asking me to spend the night, to which I gleefully responded, "Yes, can't wait!" Eventually tiring of the game, I called it quits, but the way it was played got subtly worse.

I inadvertently learned one day that I was the chart-topper of a class list, the "I Hate Sherry Club." Long before the days of instructing kids and parents on the definition of bullying and its ramifications, I dealt with the knowledge of this so-called group (consisting of girls in my homeroom I had known throughout elementary school, years before Lesa arrived) daily, knowing that I could not go to my teacher. She was probably a VIP member. My mom threatened to call Lesa's mother when she found out about the matter; Lesa was the founder and president of "the club." But I knew full well where that would get me: crucified. My next-door neighbor, Judy, had informed me that her mother, Mrs. Jones, and Mrs. Woods communicated quite frequently through the Baptist party line about the little conniving Presbyterian on the block. Nope. A phone call would only make more trouble for me. So, I stuck it out, pretending I didn't know of such things, until one day a light was thrown on the subject in one of the most depressing areas in the school, the fifth-grade girls' bathroom.

Within the dingy walls of its matching gray and mauve-pink stalls, a friend stepped forth while washing our hands after recess. Allison Bennett loudly announced to the bathroom, crowded full of girls from our class, "Lesa, I don't want to be in your club anymore." With my hands still stuck under the faucet, I turned to witness Lesa's face burn red, and my first thought was, "At least she's got the decency to blush." I didn't let on that I knew what Allison was talking about, but I was wowed by my friend's loyalty—something that can be scarce among girls of a certain age. We marched back to class without preamble, but I knew the spell had been broken; Lesa wasn't invincible. Of course, Mrs. Belden continued to adore her ass-kissing ways, naïve to the tongue behind her back, while continuing to butt heads openly with me.

One day, just prior to taking a test, I sat absent-mindedly watching my neighboring classmate, Jimmy, number his paper as we had been instructed. Mrs. Belden, busy with someone at her desk and annoyed by the noise in the room, looked up and barked, "Sherry, quit talking. Come to the desk at the front of the room." I was shocked; it was the first time I had been falsely accused by a teacher. Without given a chance to plead my innocence, I was being sentenced to the designated chair in front of the class facing the blackboard, a spot usually reserved for a kid named Ricky. She went back to her task at hand as I sat there in stunned silence. And as I sat there, a fire began to burn somewhere in my brain: *I'll be damned if I'm going to the front of the classroom.* As classmates, including Lesa, began to smile and look at me with either, *"She's going to get it,"* or *"I can't believe she's just going to sit there,"* the fire in my brain burned on. I quietly made up my mind, if sent to the office of our revered stern principal, I would walk out of that classroom in total defiance, ready to give Mr. Scott my account of the witch I had suffered under all year. She must have realized her mistake or sensed my willful stance, because she let the matter go. Nevertheless, I did not forget it and kept my back up against that woman the rest of the year. From then on, really.

Sometime during the winter of either my fifth- or sixth-grade year, my aunt came to stay with us temporarily after cracking her pelvis on the ice while on her way to catch the bus. Still young enough to be enamored over a house guest for longer than a weekend, I was also taken by her injury and the recuperation process. I had always fantasized over the use of crutches with a cast that everybody could sign, so watching my aunt manipulate her crutches around the house was thrilling. I still remember the tremors that ran through me when she described the pain she endured when (as prescribed by the physician), she would put both feet down bearing her full weight on the fractured side. She would then go to bed early, stressing her need to ease the pain with rest.

My parents had given up their bedroom so my aunt could easily access the bathroom attached to their room. It was in the same blue-tiled half-bath where I gave my dog a drink every night—not exactly straight from the faucet. My dog Hector was a small, tangled long-hair, half-breed of some sort, and I marveled at the way he would drink daintily from the Dixie cup full of water placed before him. One night, while my aunt sat on the couch suffering from a head cold, I relayed the proud feat of Hector, to my mom's and aunt's chagrin. She, unknowingly, had been sharing her Dixie cup with Hector and blamed him for all her bad cold symptoms!

• • • •

During my aunt's recuperation in our home, I can't recall that I discussed my fifth-grade heartaches, but my aunt's path would someday cross with Mrs. Belden's, though neither would ever know the other, least of all their connection with me.

• • • •

My aunt had smoked for as long as I had known her, had lived in the same white framed bungalow in South Oak Cliff in Dallas for as long as well, but the two would someday separate for good. Almost thirty years past my fifth-grade year, my aunt was diagnosed with lung cancer—not a shock to anyone, because cancer and emphysema had plagued my mother's side of the family. My aunt had always smoked cigarettes without filters and had smoked heavily. She smoked Benson and Hedges; Bill smoked Chesterfields, which were never with filters; and who knows what Raymond smoked. After my dad quit smoking, he would run around the house with a can of Lysol, trying to clear the air of stale cigarette smell after one of my aunt's visits—alone or married.

I had moved away during the time of her diagnosis and treatment, but, according to Mom, everything went fine and without major complications. That news itself was hard to digest, because my training in medical school had left me with a glum outlook on lung cancer and its definitive treatment, particularly in a long-term smoker. Things rocked along until Mom began telling me of Aunt Mary's declining health and her persistent back pains. I attributed it to metastatic lung cancer, though the physician never verified this, according to my mom. But it did come to the point, cancer or not, when my aunt required continual care in her home. So, my mom and her oldest brother, Uncle John, took weekly turns, assisting my aunt with basic needs: cooking, keeping house and fetching her medications from the pharmacy. This went on, until both caretakers were worn to a frazzle from leaving their homes on their tagged week, driving two hours to Aunt Mary, who had increasingly become difficult to please. The rub was: she needed to be closer to one of the siblings that could oversee her care, since everyone was in this for the duration of her declining medical course. As her energy flagged in the face of physical deterioration, her stubborn will to remain at home eventually yielded to the reality of the situation: she needed round-the-clock care. Whether she realized the inevitability of her forthcoming death, I could not say, but she relented nevertheless to being moved closer to my mother.

Two blocks removed from my elementary school, on a street I had walked past almost daily on my way to and from school, my mother located a private assisted-living arrangement in a well-kept red brick home. My father regularly referred to homeowners in this neighborhood as "living on silk-stocking row." There were two to three others living in the home under the auspice of a certified caregiver who cooked for them, assisted with basic living needs and essentially ran the house. Home health and hospice care was on an individual basis as set up and maintained by the resident and his or her family; if memory serves, this particular home may have only taken female residents. My mother sought care for my aunt through the local non-profit hospice, and a hospital bed was ordered for my aunt who began receiving care in a front bedroom, looking out on houses across the street where once my school playmates had lived.

The nurse, who called my mother on the night of her death, said the bedsheets were undisturbed; she had died during her sleep. I had only visited my aunt once in the early fall, before she passed peacefully that November. On the day of my visit, the leaves were beginning to turn and some were gently falling. I walked through the foyer of the home and began looking at the photos in frames arranged around the living areas. This was someone's private residence as well, and their living memories were everywhere. As I began to look closer at the framed groupings of family, primarily pictures of sisters and their brother, I began to recognize faces. One picture featured our old church organist at the Presbyterian church from my childhood: Mrs. Imogene Belden and her husband. A wonderful woman with an infectious smile and gracious countenance had been married to my fifth-grade teacher's brother, and I had never made the connection.

So, here I was in the private home of Miss Belden. When I mentioned the pictures to the vicarious caretaker, she laughed and said, "Yes, there were some good times had within these walls!"

Miss Gladice Belden was second to the youngest daughter born to Ora J. Belden and Margaret Priscilla Mudd McFarland in 1911. She was one of four daughters and two sons born to her parents; her mother and father had both been married previously with children from those unions as well. Her mother, born in Missouri, had been a descendent of the Mudd family from Maryland. I remember various times in class when Miss Belden would drone on about some connection with Roger Mudd, then the weekend and substitute weeknight news anchor for the *CBS Evening News;* whether she was referring to direct lineage, I wasn't paying enough attention to say. Apparently, three of the four daughters had never married and remained very close to one another. According to the housekeeper, the girls loved to entertain socially in the home. They enjoyed the company of each other and their mutual friends, loved their cards, smoke and drink: "Women that loved a good time," is what she called them. Well, that certainly explained a lot.

Once, while we were working in class on an assignment, Miss Belden was at her desk instructing a student independently. She looked up and said in a haggard voice, "Lauren, put all that crap away," to a friend of mine who had been messing with wads of paper she had cleaned-out from her desk. There was an on-the-spot-moment, all-class-orchestrated response, "UUHMMM!" In the 1970s elementary grade class at Wakefield Elementary, she might as well have dropped the F-bomb. She kind of laughed at herself and said, "Oh, it's not that bad of a word. You know what I mean." I didn't understand at the time that she had given me a peek into a side of herself that was far removed from the daily grind of teaching students who believed she was outdated and non-relevant. She had taught all her adult life and now as retirement was in sight (as was common to many schoolteachers during the days before teaching geared toward standardized tests), she was enduring classrooms of young students progressing toward rapidly changing times that most likely displeased her, possibly amused her, yet fascinated us.

The caretaker told me how she loved taking care of "Miss Gladice"—how she liked to pamper her, paint her fingernails and dote on her. She was not only very protective of her, but received a sense of fun and joy being around her; of all things, Miss Belden often made her laugh! Miss Gladice's mind and memories were being rearranged and misted over by dementia. She was a little disoriented at times but remained content in her home, though she might not always recognize it as such.

I sat down at the round kitchen table in front of a large bay window, looking out on the back patio, covered in leaves falling from the yard's large trees. Miss Belden was escorted to the table in her pink robe and slippers and sat in a chair right beside me. She was so close, I could see the violet shade of her painted nails. The house caregiver began fixing her breakfast after introducing me as one of her former students, a fact that seemed to skip right past her. She began commenting about the leaves outside and made small talk to me and then sometimes to no one in particular. And then, she turned directly to me and asked some question I don't even remember, due in part to *that look*. It came rushing back from the past, emblazoned on my memory from one difficult year. Those dark eyes, whose irises were hard to distinguish from the pupils, those bushy dark eyebrows drawn closer together by the furrow between them, bore into me and propelled me back to the intimidated, awkward fifth-grader I was while in her classroom.

Suddenly, the year was 1971, and I was seated in the cafeteria/auditorium of Wakefield Elementary on the corner of Sunset and Robin Lane. The spacious room was enclosed by brick walls on either side, except for rows of pastel multi-colored roll-out windows from top to bottom on the north end, directly facing a stage on the opposite end. Light streaming in those windows seemed to lift and carry the aroma of the fresh-prepared food from the kitchen down the halls of the school, signaling it was almost time for lunch. The large rows of tables with metal chairs were eventually replaced with long picnic-style benches; however, during my years there, the tables were arranged in columns until an assembly or program deemed they be stacked against the walls and the chairs be arranged in rows for the parents. The homeroom teacher always sat at the head of his or her table, and some poor kid had to sit next to the teacher. (Of course, the outlook all depended on whether you liked your teacher. In the fifth grade, I sat as far away as possible, at the opposite end of the long table that seemed to be built for such purpose.)

As in any school cafeteria around the country, the lunch hour was abuzz with chatter and laughter, and, if the noise level had grown to some unacceptable level, I was unaware. While in the middle of laughing and sharing some nonsense with my fellow classmates, Miss Belden strode to the end of the table, stood over us and fixed her hawkeyes on me—only me! And the drill-into-your-skull, Vincent Price–go-to-the-devil-and-burn-forever stare went on for what seemed minutes. In fact, I would look over my shoulder periodically, only to find her still standing over me, hands on her hips, laser-beaming down on my inquisitive, "What the hell?" expression with those dark bushy-browed framed eyes! After what seemed an eternity, she went back to her chair-of-state at the front of the table. *Egad!* I never knew what caused it, and she never said a word. Here I was, twenty-eight years later, and it seemed not much had changed. Only this time, she didn't know at whom she was looking—or did she?

• • • •

In the month of my birth, my aunt Mary died in the home of one of my most remembered teachers from all my years in public school. Mary Ellen Farnsworth Dollar, who had never lived in Sherman, who was not born in the same county, died in a residence on a street I traced often returning home from piano lessons after a long day at school. She died in a home where one of my classmates could have lived but was currently owned by a teacher whose name wreaked havoc not only in the halls of where she taught but in the long corridors of shared memories from time spent there. One woman who had doted on me before I was of age to remember and one woman who seemed to have it in for me for reasons unknown were thrown together due to circumstances neither could control, and I was the only common bond between the two.

Aunt Mary had endured nearly a lifetime before finding a man who loved her and was *so good to her*. She had seven years with the love of her life who showed up one day to do yard work at her modest South Oak Cliff address of 1634 Mentor Street. She remarried when she was seventy years old. I wonder if there was somebody in Miss Belden's life, an unrequited love or a relationship that meant as much but just wasn't declared at the altar. I once would have not pondered such things, but, as time moves on against the will and without permission, "perspectives change," as my grandmother once told me. Or, maybe, circumstances and events bring us all full circle to people in our lives who played significant roles beyond our understanding. They spring back from memory on unexpected days, causing me to take another look and give thanks somehow for all the mishaps that have weaved themselves into this tapestry of life I call mine.

About the Author

Sherry Scott, M.D., is a pediatrician who has practiced palliative/hospice care for children and general medicine. She self-published her first literary work, *The Year My Mother Died*, 2011. She founded Paris Poets Society and published a juried anthology of poetry and photography: *What Brings You Here*, 2016. She serves on the board of the Gendercide Awareness Project, founded in Dallas, Texas. She resides with her family in Paris, Texas.

Thank you so much for reading one of our **Biography / Memoirs**.
If you enjoyed our book, please check out our recommended title for your next great read!

Z.O.S. by Kay Merkel Boruff

"...dazzling in its specificity and intensity."

–C.W. Smith, author of *Understanding Women*

View other Black Rose Writing titles at www.blackrosewriting.com/books
and use promo code **PRINT** to receive a **20% discount** when purchasing.

www.ingramcontent.com/pod-product-compliance
Lightning Source LLC
Chambersburg PA
CBHW052051070526
44584CB00017B/2134